THE COMPLETE GUIDE TO
REDUCING
STRESS

THE COMPLETE GUIDE TO
REDUCING
STRESS

The natural approach

C H R I S S I E W I L D W O O D

PIATKUS

Acknowledgements

Many thanks to Howard Crabbe (horticulturalist) for advising on suitable plants for the Healing Garden, and Terry Ellis (music tutor) for his valuable input to the Voice Workshop section and for correcting the relevant part of the manuscript. I would also like to thank Anne Lawrance and Gill Cormode of Piatkus for their belief in the book and for encouraging me to finish it in reasonable time!

© 1997 Chrissie Wildwood

First published in 1997 by
Judy Piatkus (Publishers) Ltd
5 Windmill Street, London W1P 1HF

First paperback edition 1997

The moral right of the author has been asserted

A catalogue record for this book
is available from the British Library

ISBN 0-7499-1655-9 hbk
0-7499-1592-7 pbk

Edited by Carol Franklin
Designed by Chris Warner
Artwork by Tamara Sternberg

Set in Stempel Garamond by
Wyvern Typesetting Ltd, Bristol
Printed and bound in Great Britain by
The Bath Press PLC, Bath

Contents

'Men' said the Little Prince, 'set out on their way in express trains, but they do not know what they are looking for. Then they rush about, and get excited, and turn round and round ... And', he added 'it is not worth the trouble ... what they are looking for could be found in one single rose, or in a little water ... but the eyes are blind. One must look with the heart.'

ANTOINE DE SAINT-EXUPÉRY,
The Little Prince

Introduction

IF YOU were asked to list the necessities of life, what would you include? Even though it can tempting to set down numerous things, in fact we have relatively few essential needs. Basically, we need fresh air, clean water, nourishing food, good hygiene, protective clothing, shelter, adequate exercise, nurturing and a sense of freedom. Equally, we need communion with the natural world. For nature in her myriad forms is a potent de-stresser and healer of the soul – a simple fact so often overlooked by experts in the field of 'stress management'. Nature offers tranquillity to the frenzied, replenishes the energy of the depleted and uplifts the spirits of everyone. All that is demanded in return is a little of our time and attention.

Even if you can only occasionally leave the city to visit the countryside, sea or mountains (or if you cannot get away at all), do not despair. As you are about to discover, the healing spirit of nature stirs within the most humble of places: the local park; an urban sunset; a dandelion growing through a pavement crack; a window box full of geraniums; the purring of a cat; and the chirping of a scruffy city sparrow! The secret key to inner peace and harmony is to become consciously aware of such things, to lose yourself in the sensations of the moment. This state of relaxed yet focused awareness is the essence of meditation, the basic techniques of which are explored in Chapter 1. However, since stress reduction is the main theme of this book (and therefore embraced in every chapter), let us establish what exactly we mean by stress.

THE NATURE OF STRESS

Stress is often defined as a single identifiable ailment associated with the 'fight or flight' hormone, adrenaline. This hormone prepares the individual to resist ('fight') or avoid ('flight') attack. In modern life, however, it is not always possible to deal with stress in this way, and so we bottle up our true feelings. And, as a result, there is no direct outlet for the physical and emotional effects of adrenaline. The longer the 'stressed out' feeling remains, the more harmful it can be.

The effects of stress may be experienced within any part of the mind/body complex, depending upon our own innate physical and emotional constitution. One common symptom of prolonged stress is a weakening of the immune defences, resulting in fatigue, a susceptibility to every passing infection and allergies. Stress can also trigger skin problems (or exacerbate an existing condition) such as acne and eczema. And should it affect the respiratory system, we may suffer congestion and hay fever. We also know that stress raises blood pressure and is a contributing factor in the development of heart disease. It can also play havoc with the endocrine and reproductive systems, manifesting perhaps as severe PMS, low fertility (in men and women), thyroid dysfunction, maturity onset diabetes, and a whole host of other complaints.

Having painted such a bleak picture, it is important to get everything into perspective. The idea that stress is all bad is a misunderstanding. Unlike sheep, humans need a high amount of stimulation to motivate us and keep us going. It sharpens our senses and helps us adapt to our environment. Indeed, without the 'spice of life' we begin to feel downhearted. Stress only becomes a problem when it develops into *di*stress, especially if the feeling is prolonged.

Whether we are suffering from the strain of living in the fast track, or the burden of a monotonous existence, in either situation we feel we have absolutely no control over our life, and we *fear* there is no way out. Even though the spectrum of human emotion may seem infinitely broad, according to the American stress expert Dr C. Norman Shealy, there are just four major feeling of distress, and each stems from an attitude of *fear*, namely: anxiety, anger, guilt and depression. All other negative feelings are actually synonyms of these four.

As for the 'stress', this was borrowed from the language of engineering, meaning 'any force upon an object which causes strain in that object' (for example, when designing a bridge the engineer must ascertain the maximum weight and vibration the bridge will tolerate before collapsing under the strain). However, this definition is inadequate when applied to human beings. In truth, it is not so much the outside pressures and problems which impinge upon us, but rather what happens inside us as we react to those things or people 'out there'. For instance, we all know people who remain cool, calm and collected under the most trying circumstances, and we know others who collapse under the strain of even relatively minor difficulties. Then there are those who are blessed with an exceptionally resilient constitution. Such individuals may flout all the rules of healthy eating and a balanced lifestyle, and yet appear to enjoy emotional and physical equilibrium. None the less, the secret of maintaining a sense of well-being is to find just the right level of stimulation and relaxation to make life interesting and fulfilling, and of course this balance is different for each individual.

The Stress Assessment Questionnaire

Many traditional sources of stress management demand the completion of certain stress assessment questionnaires designed to measure the impact of specific life events upon our health and well-being. Any life change, whether positive or negative, is said to trigger a degree of stress. The popular Social Readjustment Rating Scale (devised by the American doctors T.H. Holmes and R.G. Rahe), cites 41 life events, each of which is valued according to the surmised amount of adjustment needed to cope with the experience. The death of a spouse, for example, scores the maximum of 100 points (even though the death of a child may be at least, if not more traumatic, this event is not included in the original research), divorce scores 73, marriage 50 and Christmas 12. A medium to high score of 150 to 300 points threatens a '50/50 chance of a major health problem in the next two years'. A very high score of over 300 points does not bear thinking about.

Without wishing to condemn this approach completely out of hand (it probably serves some useful purpose), it has to be acknowledged that it takes little imagination for such foreboding

statistics to engender further distress. Indeed, in my work as an aromatherapist and flower remedy consultant I have encountered this problem many times. Worse still, having sown the seed of fear (even though that fear may have become buried in the unconscious), it may well take root and develop into a self-fulfilling prophesy. Without doubt, the 'mind over matter' phenomenon is very real and can manifest for good or ill. Quite apart from anything else, the statistical approach to assessing individual stress levels is seriously flawed. It overlooks the all-important idiosyncratic nature of stress-related illness. While too much (or too little) stress in our lives can indeed deplete our adaptive resources, it is also true that one person's stressor is another's passport to freedom.

THE GENTLE APPROACH

With the current plethora of books on the subject of stress, it would seem appropriate at this juncture to pose the question, 'What makes this book different?'. Taking an holistic approach, it explores the ways in which we may strengthen our own innate self-healing ability. Even though some people are born more resilient than others, most of us can greatly improve our health and foster a more positive outlook. The key to enhanced well-being lies in the realisation that we need not become helpless victims of stress.

To a large extent, of course, our health is dependent on the quality of food we eat, the water we drink and the air we breathe. Perhaps even more importantly, we need to nurture the spiritual aspect of our being, for we are more than a body and a mind. Even when we do not follow a conscious spiritual path in terms of a religious faith, we may in fact be embracing the spiritual aspect of 'self' (that which is aware of our true purpose in life) in some other way. It could be through a love of music or some other art form, no matter how humble, or simply through our work, family, relationships, or through a love of animals or nature – or more actively perhaps by working towards the realisation of a humanitarian or Green ideal.

Without losing sight of the spiritual thread, this book offers many gentle and imaginative ways to relax and revitalise, to find inner peace and healing – not only through nature as encountered in the great outdoors, but in a broader context to include a wide range of soul-caressing pursuits.

Chapter 1 begins with the rhythm of life – the ebbing and flowing of the tides, the waxing and waning of the moon, the changing seasons – and our own deep connection with cycles of nature. It also introduces the art of deep breathing, conscious relaxation and meditation; and reveals the joys of inner space music, voice work and free expressive dance.

Chapter 2 takes a closer look at emotion and our sense of purpose and meaning. The Bach flower remedies are introduced, together with advice on choosing and using these gentle remedies for healing emotional disharmony. Also included are exercises for discharging pent-up emotion – the root cause of many physical ills. Then we move into the intriguing world of creating mood-enhancing room scents using essential oils. There is also a section on the therapeutic properties of colour, followed by an introduction to art therapy through the ancient practice of mandala work.

The ways in which we may promote health and vitality from the grass roots, as it were, are explored in Chapter 3. Advice is given on such things as healthy eating, mood foods, yoga, therapeutic bathing and skin brushing. There is also a step-by-step guide to the art of aromatherapy massage for body and soul.

Nature lovers will be especially interested in Chapter 4, for here we encounter the spirit of place – an energy that can be called upon to heal a troubled soul. This section also offers novel exercises for enhancing sensory perception while communing with nature. It is by developing our ability to look, listen, smell, taste, touch and imagine that we begin to experience exalted states of awareness.

According to the ancients, when we invite beauty into our homes, we embrace every level of our being. So Chapter 5 offers ideas for creating a healing environment, employing such things as natural room scents, pollution-eating houseplants and garden plants for the soul. It also introduces the ancient Chinese art of placement – feng shui – for promoting physical, emotional and spiritual harmony.

Chapter 6 gives advice on employing the imagination for reducing stress levels and promoting personal happiness. Included in this section is a guided imagery exercise which can be recorded on to tape.

The final chapter considers how we might capture the time to enjoy such life-enhancing pursuits; for time is an elusive commodity in this world of speed, deadlines and dutiful activity.

As you can see, this book covers a broad spectrum of life-enhancing practices. However, it is not expected that you should work through everything systematically. Rather, you are encouraged to concentrate on what you *enjoy* doing rather than what you believe *ought* to be good for you. As far as this book is concerned, there is no truth in the age-old belief that a certain amount of discomfort must be felt if it is to do us any good. On the contrary, the more wonderful the experience, the more healing the effect – and the more likely you will be to keep it up.

Indeed, my approach to health and healing has moved from a strict adherence to all that is 'right' in terms of lifestyle and diet, to the realisation that we can be very much more flexible than some health gurus would have us believe. In fact, the philosophy of the healing power of pleasure is nothing new. It was shared by the ancient Greek physician Asclepiades, who advocated nurturing massage, aromatic baths, flowers, music, beautiful art objects and perfume to soothe away the stresses and strains of life – even wine had a place in his Elysian regime!

Nevertheless, it would be folly to throw all caution to the wind: to smoke, consume excessive quantities of alcohol, or exist entirely on junk food to our heart's discontent. Equally, however, to live a self-righteous life of raw carrots, fruit juice and prolonged meditation can be just as harmful. Even though the true ascetic does exist, the average person's spirit cries out to experience life to the full. Interestingly, there is an Eastern school of thought whose adherents practise 'mystical hedonism' – a technique employing the full use of the senses to overcome the senses – as a means to attaining 'higher' states of consciousness. Indeed, there are many roads to spiritual fulfilment, so why traverse the most difficult when you can walk the primrose path?

Unless there is a serious underlying health problem which stands a good chance of being corrected by certain dietary and lifestyle disciplines (under the guidance of a qualified health practitioner), it would seem nonsensical to make life more difficult than it need be. People who inflict a harsh regime on themselves, whether it be through spartan diet, compulsive exercise, perfectionism, or whatever, must be gluttons for punishment – or fearful of moving with natural ebb and flow of life.

Of course, there are those who have been dealt a harsh card through poverty, chronic ill health or a life-time of suffering in one form or another – the 'higher' reasons for which I do not pretend to understand fully, nor to accept graciously. Therefore, I will not attempt to offer an 'all-knowing' explanation bound up with past life theory, karma ('As ye sow, so shall ye reap') or other metaphysical explanation for suffering and disease.

THE ESSENCE OF TRUE HEALING

Since the word 'healing' appears frequently throughout this book, it would seem appropriate to establish what exactly is meant by this. Contrary to what many believe, to be healed is not necessarily about the disappearance of physical symptoms. Indeed, the pathological condition may have progressed beyond all possibility of treatment, barring a miracle. And yet we can still become healed in a spiritual sense. The experience of healing manifests as a new-found (or renewed) sense of purpose and meaning to life, accompanied by a feeling of inner ease. Those who care for the terminally ill within the hospice movement would agree that it is the relinquishment of our old enemy *fear* which frees the spirit and enables us to die happy and at peace with ourselves, with others, and the world about us. And this is the essence of *true* healing.

THE NATURAL SCHEME OF THINGS

It is also important to acknowledge that a state of fearlessness or emotional equilibrium is virtually impossible to attain as a permanent state of being. Yogis and great spiritual teachers may have achieved such an ideal, but most of us will be held in check from time to time in response to the ups and downs of life, especially potentially life-shattering events as bereavement, divorce or any other great loss. Indeed, it would be self-destructive and inhuman not to express our distress in such circumstances for suppressed emotional pain eats away at the soul. Likewise, the earth may quake and erupt, and blow and storm, for this is the natural scheme of things.

THE SIMPLE JOYS OF LIFE

What better way to invoke the healing power of nature than to indulge your sensuous feelings – feelings that will transport you to higher realms. So, whenever you can, breathe in the scents of flowers, trees and grasses; listen to the birds, moving water or the moaning wind; touch the rough bark of an ancient tree; contemplate the beauty of your favourite animal; walk barefoot on the seashore with the wind on your skin and the saltspray on your lips; and taste the first strawberries of summer.

And if you are physically able, the ultimate way to commune with nature is to head for the wilds. There is something special about climbing a mountain, especially for the first time, or swimming in a clean river, or camping on the edge of forest, or rambling on the high moors. Even in winter, do not be afraid of the wind and rain, snow or frost. Wrap up warmly so that you need not hunch up against the cold. Relax and enjoy it! There is something special indeed, something mystical yet profoundly real about coming close to the earth.

As well as helping you to reduce stress the natural way, I trust this book will encourage you to nurture every aspect of your being. And in so doing, I hope it will open your heart to the simple joys of life.

CHRISSIE WILDWOOD
Autumn 1996

1

The Rhythm of Life

*E*MERGING from the cosmic chaos are spirals of organised vibration or rhythm. Rhythm has to do with repetition and cycles: the changing seasons – spring and summer, autumn and winter; the rhythms of day and night; inhalation and exhalation; birth and death. Indeed, the entire universe can be defined in terms of vibrations, rhythms and waves; patterns of expansiveness and contraction which are implicit in every process.

Women have always recognised their own cyclic nature in the moon, their periodicity being measured in 28-day cycles corresponding to the lunar phases. We are also influenced by a daily or 'circadian' cycle, a biological clock which governs many psychophysiological processes, including sleep, periods of mental alertness, and fluctuations in body weight and albumen content of the urine.

Naturopathy (the treatment of illness without drugs involving such measures as diet, exercise, massage and salt baths) and oriental systems of healing recognise that we are especially influenced by the changing seasons. In winter the body generates maximum internal heat by raising the metabolic rate; and thus there is an inclination to eat more, particularly warming foods like stews and heavy puddings. However, we may also feel somewhat sluggish and inclined to sleep for longer periods. Come the spring and the production of body heat gradually subsides; we feel lighter and more energetic. We may also favour a diet that is less stodgy or fatty than during the winter months. By midsummer, especially if the weather is very hot, appetite and energy output decreases and we are inclined to feel sleepy during the midday period. We are also likely to prefer cool food and drink. An unhealthy body, however, adapts less efficiently to the changing seasons, perhaps generating too much heat in summer and too little in winter. The most problematic times are during the transitional phases of early spring and autumn. Many people experience increased susceptibility to coughs and colds during these periods, or an exacerbation of an existing health problem – a phenomenon which is also recognised in conventional medicine.

GAIA

Taking a broader perspective, the British scientist James Lovelock and his American colleague Lynn Margulis, in the mid-1970s, conceived of the Gaia hypothesis (a name from Greek mythology for the goddess of earth). In the Gaia theory, the earth is far more than than a mass of rock, water and gases spinning aimlessly through space; it is an infinitely complex, evolving entity, constantly striving for balance – an organic system of which we ourselves are a part. (This 'living earth' realisation has been embraced by mystics and philosophers for thousands of years.) Tragically, like a body overburdened with the debris of an unhealthy existence, our planet is suffering from the most severe strain. Rainforests are being destroyed at an alarming rate; deserts are advancing; water, soil and air are being degraded and polluted. Like ourselves, Gaia can adapt to potentially harmful changes, but only within certain limits. Should those limits be surpassed, Gaia dies. Quite a sobering thought.

But all is not lost. We need to envision a future where such qualities of compassion, intuition and nurturing – qualities which are part and parcel of the philosophy of holistic healing and within the Green movement in general – have become integral to human consciousness as a whole. Such awareness fosters the humbling realisation that humanity does not have absolute dominion over the earth – for we are a species among many – and that we and Gaia move together.

It is by becoming aware of the rhythms of nature that we learn to harmonise with the spirit of Gaia – and with our own spiritual essence. The spiritual aspect of 'self' is hard to define, but is tied up with our relationship with ourselves, with other people and with our sense of purpose and meaning – and not least with our sense of the transcendent. In this way we can begin to find inner peace and the ability to deal with the stresses of life. However, we shall return to this subject later. In the mean time, let us explore some of the ways in which we may experience for ourselves the healing power of rhythm. And what better place to begin than with the breath of life?

THE BREATH

The process of taking in oxygen and eliminating poisonous wastes is essential to life. Therefore, any problem with breathing will affect the whole mind/body complex, possibly leading to a susceptibility to every passing infection, along with feelings of anxiety, despondency or depression.

As an aromatherapist, one of the most common problems reported to me is perpetual tiredness; and this is usually perceived as resulting from stress. When we feel stressed the amount of energy expended is so great that it almost always leads to an energy deficit. By learning to influence our breathing, however, we can alter our energy levels and our mood.

To illustrate this, start to breathe shallowly; pant in and out very quickly for about half a minute. At the end of this time you will feel decidedly anxious – your heart will be pounding and you may even be experiencing fear. To allay any discomfort, take three or four long, deep breaths from the abdomen and exhale slowly. You will find your mind and body sinking into a state of calm. From this it may be easier to understand just why deep breathing can induce both tranquillity and revitalisation at the same moment.

Harnessing the Life-Force

In humanity's quest for healing and self-knowledge, the power of the breath has become associated with an energy of a metaphysical kind; an energy which could be defined as the subtle life principle permeating the universe. As touched upon earlier, this idea corresponds broadly to that of modern nuclear physics, which regards all matter (including the human body) as energy or vibration organised in different ways. To the Chinese, who attempt to manipulate it in acupuncture, it is *chi*; to the Australian Aborigine it is *kuranita*; to the Polynesian, *manas*; to the yogi, it is *prana*.

Those who practise yoga will also be familiar with the term *pranayama*, which is the harnessing of this vital energy by means of certain breathing exercises. Although *prana* is manifest everywhere in the universe, the most important source is the air we breathe. Indeed, we can exist for some time without food, a shorter time without water, but without air we die within minutes.

If we relate the theories of yoga to Western science we may conclude that *prana* is composed, if not completely at least fundamentally, of electrically charged particles known as negative ions. Negative ions are abundant wherever the air is fresh and clean. They enhance a sense of well-being by reducing fatigue and hypertension, which in turn has a positive effect on the body's immune defences. (The study of the power of the mind and its influence over the immune system is grounded in the new science of *psychoneuroimmunology* – PNI for short!)

Conversely, where there is an abundance of positive ions (those with an absence of electrons) we begin to feel devitalised. Postive ions are generated in polluted environments. Moreover, electrical sources such as heaters and appliances, domestic and industrial, generate their own electrical fields and produce postive ions in the immediate atmosphere.

However, nature is not adverse to generating her own positive ions, for example, in wind currents associated with earthquakes and volcanic eruptions, and during high velocity winds accompanied by sudden temperature increases and drops in humidity. Such weather changes are known to trigger degrees of emotional and physical disharmony, problems such as headaches and irritability, and even biochemical changes such as preventing the proper coagulation of the blood. For this reason, some doctors in Switzerland do not operate during a windstorm!

The Benefits of Deep Breathing

Deep breathing promotes health and vitality. It is also a prerequisite to the art of conscious relaxation, meditation and creative imagery (the practice of creative imagery is explored in Chapter 6). Moreover, the ability to breathe deeply and fully is an excellent stress-reducing technique in its own right.

Unfortunately, many of us are shallow breathers; we use only the upper part of our lungs, which means that toxic residues are not completely removed. While shallow breathing contributes to low vitality, conversely it often develops as a result of ill health. Poor breathing is also associated with sedentary living, faulty posture and a build-up of nervous tension. Apart from regular practice of the breathing exercises suggested in this chapter, good breathing is fostered through physical activity (preferably in the fresh air) such as walking, cycling, tennis, football and so forth. Swimming is another beneficial form of movement which even those of advanced age can enjoy. Quite apart from stimulating optimum functioning of the lungs, *enjoyable* exercise causes the release of certain neuro-hormones such as endorphins and encephalins, which are the body's natural opiates or 'happiness chemicals'.

One of the finest breathing exercises is the yoga Complete Breath (see pages 15–16). This technique is especially beneficial to sufferers of respiratory ailments such as asthma, hay fever and bronchitis. However, it can also be of enormous benefit to those who cannot take vigorous exercise, perhaps because of ill health (including chronic tiredness), or advanced age. Most important, it encourages breathing through the nose, rather than the mouth.

Even though mouth breathing has its uses – it is encouraged by certain therapists as a means to releasing pent-up emotion – it is not the ideal way to breathe in general. Nose breathing ensures that the air is filtered by the nasal hairs which trap large dust particles. These particles, when swallowed, can exacerbate a tendency to produce excessive mucus or catarrh. Of course, the hairs in the nose cannot filter out noxious substances like carbon monoxide and industrial pollutants. None the less, yoga teachers assure us that the purifying and energising benefits of correct breathing will outweigh the unavoidable inhalation of polluted air.

If you are to practise your breathing exercises indoors, you may wish to enhance the process by vaporising an appropriate essential oil. Each of the essences listed below has a special affinity with the respiratory system, helping to clear excessive mucus and encouraging deeper breathing. Essential oils also help to purify the air, for almost all are powerful slayers of air-borne microbes. Choose an oil (or a blend of two or three) according to your aroma preference. (*Instructions for vaporising essential oils are to be found on page 56.*)

SUGGESTED ESSENTIAL OILS

cajeput
cedarwood
cypress
elemi
eucalyptus
frankincense

juniperberry
myrrh
myrtle
niaouli
pine
sandalwood

In view of what was mentioned earlier about our affinity with the trees, you may be intrigued to to learn that all of these oils are extracted from various parts of trees! Moreover, frankincense, cedarwood and sandalwood have been used for centuries as sacred incense, for their enigmatic aromas are believed to lull the mind into 'higher' states of awareness.

THE COMPLETE BREATH LYING

3 Begin to breathe out slowly through your nose in a smooth continuous flow until the abdomen is drawn in and the rib-cage and chest are relaxed. Ideally, the

out-breath will take twice as long to complete as the in-breath. Hold for a few seconds before taking the next deep breath. Repeat the movement two or three times.

1 Find a quiet space where you will not be disturbed for at least ten minutes. Loosen any tight clothing around your chest and waist, and remove your shoes. Lie on a rug on the floor (or the ground if outside, perhaps in a garden), or alternatively on a firm bed, with your arms at your sides, several centimetres away from your body, palms facing down. If you have a weak back, you will find it more comfortable to place a couple of pillows under your knees. A thin pillow or a folded towel can be placed under your head to support your neck if you wish.

2 Close your eyes and begin to inhale very slowly through your nose. Expand your rib-cage, and then your chest. Your abdomen will be automatically drawn in as the ribs move out and the chest expands.

Important: Never force the breath by straining. After a week or so of regular practice your ribs will expand more easily, thus allowing the air to flow through the lungs smoothly and rhythmically.

4 Now breathe in slowly as you did in Step 1 but gradually raise your arms overhead in time with the inhalation until the backs of your hands touch the floor (see below). By raising and lowering the arms as you inhale and exhale, you encourage the diaphragm (the dome-like muscle between the chest and the abdominal cavity) to work more efficiently. In diaphragmatic breathing, air is pulled down into the lower lungs, where most of the blood circulates.

5 Having filled your lungs with air, hold your breath for a few seconds while you have a good stretch, from fingertips to toes.

6 Slowly breathe out as you bring your arms back down to your sides. Repeat two or three times.

Step 4

THE COMPLETE BREATH STANDING

The benefits of this exercise are the same as for the previous exercise, but you may wish to try out both movements in order to discover for yourself which is easiest to perform.

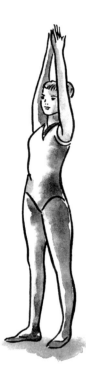

1 Stand with your back straight, head erect and your feet slightly apart.

2 Inhale through your nose slowly and deeply, and at the same time raise your arms up until your palms meet above your head. Hold the breath for a few seconds while you have a good stretch.

3 Exhale slowly as you lower the arms back down to your sides. Repeat the movement six to eight times.

THE 'HA' BREATH

1 Stand with your back straight, head erect and feet slightly apart (see left).

2 Inhale through your nose slowly and deeply, as you raise your arms backwards over your head.

3 Hold the breath for a moment.

4 Allow your arms and upper part of your body to fall forward, with your knees bent to prevent strain in your back, and at the same time throw out the breath through your mouth with a 'Ha' sound.

During periods of inactivity, especially when we are asleep, toxins build up in the stomach and lungs. With the 'Ha' breath, these impurities are thrown out more effectively. This movement will also dissipate nervous tension, as the body does naturally when we feel the urge to sigh. Although the 'Ha' breath is traditionally performed first thing in the morning, it can also be practised whenever you feel in need of a pick-me-up. It will refresh your whole system.

5 Inhale slowly as you raise your body into a standing position. Repeat the exercise two or three times.

DEEP RELAXATION

Having mastered the Complete Breath, which should take no longer than a week of regular practice, you may wish to experience deep relaxation. Indeed, it is advisable to become accustomed to deep breathing before you begin conscious relaxation, especially if you have been under stress for some time. Prolonged stress results in habitual shallow breathing with all its ill effects. Until this is remedied, a state of deep relaxation is extremely difficult to achieve.

However, there is another aspect which is rarely acknowledged: if we do manage to reach a state of deep relaxation, despite having been under prolonged pressure, this can be quite a shock to the system. Negative feelings may come to the surface, feelings which hitherto were kept under strict control. For when we are addicted to a manic lifestyle, all too often it is a way of avoiding coming to terms with some form of pain or loss. Or it could be a deep-rooted fear of coming face to face with ourselves, warts and all. Indeed, this can feel awkward to say the least. So to avoid any unpleasant surprises, it is vital to take things slowly, to master deep breathing before moving on. In so doing, any negative feelings that may surface are no more than you can deal with at the time.

As well as dissipating excessive nervous energy and promoting serenity, studies in hospitals have shown that deep relaxation improves sleep, lowers high blood pressure, releases tension in the muscles, improves digestion, helps certain skin complaints and strengthens the immune system.

Deep relaxation is most beneficial if practised once a day (twice a day if you have time) for the first two weeks, and three or four times a week thereafter. It is advisable to wait at least an hour after eating before each relaxation session, otherwise most of your energy will be concentrated in the digestive processes, thus hindering the relaxation response. On the other hand, if you are feeling ravenously hungry your rumbling stomach will distract your attention!

After a few months of practising the sequence on pages 20–1, you may find that one session a week is enough. This is because the beneficial effects of deep relaxation are cumulative and familiarity with the exercise conditions the body into responding more quickly.

Enhancing the Experience

The room in which you intend to practise needs to be comfortably warm, well-ventilated and with a peaceful atmosphere. Wear loose, comfortable clothing and take off your shoes. If you live in a noisy area, it may also be helpful to play a tape or CD of gentle music, but keep the volume down very low as your senses will be especially acute. You may also wish to enhance the atmosphere by vaporising a relaxing essential oil (or a blend of two or three) chosen from those listed below. (*Instructions for vaporising essential oils are to be found on page 56.*)

SUGGESTED ESSENTIAL OILS

bergamot
chamomile (Roman)
cedarwood
clary sage
cypress
frankincense
juniper berry

lavender
mandarin
neroli
petitgrain
rose
sandalwood
vetiver

If you have a friend or partner with a pleasant voice, perhaps they could be persuaded to guide you through the following sequence – at least for a few sessions until you are familiar with the process. Or you could perhaps record the instructions on to tape – that is, if you are happy with the tone of your own voice and the quality of your recording equipment. You should make your recording on a long-playing C90 cassette. This will ensure that you are not prematurely, and rudely, awakened by the 'click' at the end. Instructions must be spoken very slowly, softly and clearly. Remember to pause after each demand to allow time for the breathing and stretching to be carried out. Most important, ensure that you will not be disturbed for at least 20 minutes.

┌─ DEEP RELAXATION ─┐ SEQUENCE

The following exercise suggests exhaling for a count of five. However, you may find, for example, that you are more comfortable with a count of four, or that you need to continue for a count of six, eight or ten. It is important to discover the rhythm that is right for you, and this may change from time to time. Remember to wear loose, comfortable clothing and to remove your shoes.

1 Lie down on the floor or on a firm bed supported by pillows if you wish – one under your head, and one or two under your knees to support your lower back.

2 Close your eyes, take a deep breath through your nose and then breathe out through your mouth with a deep sigh. Repeat two or three times. (*If you are directing this sequence for a partner remain silent for about 30 seconds before moving on the next instruction.*)

3 Now become aware of your feet. Inhale your nose, tighten your feet by pointing your toes, and then flexing your feet towards your body. Hold on to this tension for a slow count of five. (*If you are directing this sequence, it would be helpful to count out loud 'one ... two ... three ... four ... five ...'*) Now let go of your feet as you breathe out with a sigh of relief.

4 Become aware of your knees. Inhale through your nose, tighten your knees, holding on to the tension for a slow count of five. (*One ... two ... three ... four ... five ...*) Let go of your knees as you breathe out with a deep sigh.

5 Allow your attention to move into your thighs. Inhale through your nose, tighten your thighs, holding on to the tension for a slow count of five. (*One ... two ... three ... four ... five ...*). Now let go, breathing out with a sigh. Experience a wonderful sensation of release.

6 Now become aware of your buttocks. Breathe in through your nose, tighten your buttocks, holding on to the tension for a slow count of five. (*One ... two ... three ... four ... five ...*) Let go of your buttocks as you breathe out with a deep sigh of relief.

7 Allow your awareness to move into your abdomen. Inhale through your nose, pull in your abdomen and tighten those muscles. Hold on to the tension for a slow count of five. (*One ... two ... three ... four ... five ...*) And now breathe out with a deep sigh.

8 Now become aware of your chest. Inhale through your nose, tighten those chest muscles and hold for a slow count of five. (*One ... two ... three ... four ... five ...*) Now release, breathing out with a deep sigh of relief.

9 Become aware of your shoulders. Breathe in through your nose, hunch your shoulders, pulling them up towards your ears. Hold on to the tension for a slow count of five. (*One ... two ... three ... four ... five ...*) Now let go of those shoulders as you breathe out with a sigh, experiencing a wonderful sensation of release.

10 Move your attention into your hands. Breathe in through your nose, tighten your hands into fists, holding on to the tension for a slow count of five. (*One ... two ... three ... four ... five ...*) Now release your hands as you breathe out with a deep sigh.

11 Become aware of your arms. Tighten your arms, feeling the tension right down into your fingertips. Hold on to the tension for a slow count of five. (*One ... two ... three ... four ... five ...*) Let go of the tension as you breathe out with a deep sigh, feeling a wonderful sensation of release.

12 Become aware of your neck. Breathe in through your nose. Now arch your neck, holding on to the tension for a slow count of five. (*One ... two ... three ... four ... five ...*) Let go of the tension as you breathe out with a deep sigh.

13 Allow your attention to focus on your face and scalp. Take a deep breath through your nose, now clench your jaw and pull your face into a terrible grimace! Hold on to the tension for a slow count of five. (*One ... two ... three ... four ... five ...*) Now let go, breathing out through your mouth with a deep sigh. Experience a wave of relaxation moving over your whole body, from the top of your head right down into your toes. Experience a wonderful sensation of release. (*If directing this sequence, remain silent for one minute before moving on to the next instruction.*)

14 Become aware of your body again and 'feel' around in your mind for any areas that may still be tense. Repeat the tightening and releasing of muscle groups until you feel deeply relaxed. Remain in this beautiful state for a while, perfectly at ease, perfectly at peace, until you are beckoned to return to the everyday world. (*If directing this sequence, remain silent for 10 to 15 minutes before moving on to the next instruction, which must be spoken very softly so as not to startle the listener.*)

15 Now it is time to return from your inner journey. Take a deep breath and, at the same time, raise your arms overhead and have a good stretch from fingertips to toes. (*If directing, allow a few moments for this movement to be carried out before moving on to the final instruction.*)

16 When you feel ready, roll over to one side before slowly getting up.

MEDITATION

It is important to establish the difference between deep relaxation and meditation, for the two are sometimes regarded as synonymous. Deep relaxation allows the mind to drift into a pleasant dreamlike state, with no direction or focus. Meditation, on the other hand, is a state of relaxed alertness, of becoming fully focused on the sensations of the moment.

The beneficial effects of meditation are similar to those of deep relaxation, but with the additional reward of facilitating communication with the spiritual aspect of our being. In some schools of psychotherapy the human spirit is called the higher self – the all-wise aspect that manifests itself in those rare moments of inspiration and clarity; in those moments of profound insight into the real purpose of our existence.

There are many forms of meditation, some of which are way beyond the average person's capacity, requiring dedication to an extremely high degree. Other methods, such as those described in this chapter, are delightfully simple and yet highly beneficial. As the Tibetan master Soyal Rinpoche says, 'The method is only a means, not the meditation itself. It is by practising the method skilfully that you reach that pure state of total presence'.

No matter which type of meditation we may choose to embark upon, concentration is the basis of every system. However, the mind has an irritating habit of rebelling against the instructions we may give it. Eastern sages have likened the mind to a monkey, for it has a tendency to leap continually from branch to branch, following an endless pattern of activity. None the less, we can learn to quieten mental chatter, to transcend the everyday level of consciousness. As you are about to discover, the secret of quietening the mind is through gentle persuasion rather than reprimand.

Position for Meditation

Lying down is not a good position for meditation because it is associated with falling asleep; the aim of meditation is to remain alert. If you are accustomed to sitting on the floor in a cross-legged position, then by all means adopt this pose. Otherwise sit on the floor with your back supported against a wall (a cushion

placed in the small of the back will help prevent you from slumping), with your legs outstretched and feet together, and your hands resting on your thighs. Alternatively, sit in a straight-backed chair (which should support your back) with your feet flat on the floor, your hands resting in your lap. Your position needs to be comfortable, but poised in order to facilitate your breathing.

Time and Place

Try to meditate at the same time and place every day. The mind is addicted to habit. Once a pattern of meditation is established, it slips more easily into an altered state of consciousness. The ideal time to meditate is at the start of day. For one thing, the early hours are likely to be quieter, and for another, our minds are then comparatively still, not yet caught up in the maelstrom of everyday activities and demands. Above all, the dawn hour is traditionally a magical time for communication between the two realms of our being – spiritual and physical.

If morning meditation is not possible, the next best time is the sunset hour – another sacred time revered by the seers and mystics of olden times. As the sun goes down, the breathing of Gaia seems to move into a slower rhythm, and likewise the mind turns more easily inwards.

It is gratifying to know that once you have found stability in your meditation, noises and other distractions will have less impact. An experienced meditator can find inner stillness just about anywhere, even while travelling on the London Underground during the rush hour!

The space in which you intend to meditate needs to be comfortably warm, well-ventilated and pleasing to the senses. Avoid harsh overhead lighting. Opt for soft lamps or candlelight in the evening, or natural light during the day (perhaps diffused through a lightweight blind or muslin curtains). Although not essential for everyone, an inspiring picture or art object, a rock crystal or fresh flowers can be a spiritual stimulus. You may also wish to vaporise a traditional meditation oil such as frankincense, cedarwood or sandalwood. (*Instructions for vaporising essential oils are to be found on page 56.*)

Some people enjoy meditating outdoors, in a garden or a place of beauty far away from the maddening crowd. This is my own preference. However, we are all different: what works for one person may not work for another. There are those who find the sense of expansion experienced in the presence of nature inconducive to focused work.

If you lead an extremely busy life, perhaps as a parent with young children, it may well be difficult to fix a daily routine, and especially to find a quiet place where you will not be disturbed. In this case, it may be wise to postpone any aspirations in this direction, at least until the children start school. If you are determined to meditate, however, it may be just possible to steal those precious moments (see Chapter 7 for more on Finding Time).

Meditation on the Breath

This is one of the simplest ways to begin meditating. It facilitates the ability to concentrate and to move into an altered state of consciousness. As with the deep relaxation exercise, you may find it helpful to record the sequence on to tape; or perhaps to ask someone else to guide you through it until such time as you are familiar with the process and can dispense with any outside help.

It is advisable, however, to master the art of deep relaxation before you begin learning how to meditate. Without such conditioning, the relaxation response (which is essential for the process of meditation) may take much longer than the time allowed in the following sequence.

There is no need to meditate for extended periods. As little as one (perhaps two) 10 to 15-minute sessions a day will be enough to refresh your mind and replenish your energies. Initially, you may need to glance at a clock (preferably no more than once during the meditation) to remind yourself when to stop. However, once accustomed to the process you will assuredly find yourself moving out of meditation at the appointed time, without any external help. If this sounds unlikely, think back to a time when you set the bedside alarm, only to wake up the next morning within seconds of it sounding. The all-knowing unconscious aspect of mind never ceases to amaze the relatively naïve conscious self!

Remember to wear loose, comfortable clothing so as not to restrict your breathing, and remove your shoes.

SIMPLE MEDITATION ON THE BREATH

1 Close your eyes. Empty your lungs by exhaling through the mouth with a sigh. Now begin to breathe through your nose, allowing your abdomen to extend slightly with each inhalation, and to sink in again as you exhale. (*If directing this sequence, remain silent for 30 seconds.*)

2 Become aware of your feet, thinking relaxation into them (*five seconds*) ... Now move over every part of your body in turn, letting go and relaxing every part, continuing with your calves ... (*five seconds*) ... knees ... (*five seconds*) ... thighs ... (*five seconds*) ... hips ... (*five seconds*) ... abdomen ... (*five seconds*) ... now your chest ... (*five seconds*) ... hands ... (*five seconds*) ... and arms ... (*five seconds*) ... shoulders ... (*five seconds*) ... neck ... (*five seconds*) ... and now your face ... (*five seconds*) ... your eyes ... (*five seconds*) ... your forehead ... (*five seconds*) ... your scalp ... (*five seconds*) ... even your tongue ... (*five seconds*).

3 Become aware of your breath once again. Breathe naturally without strain, making absolutely no effort to control the breath. It does not matter if your breath is uneven, longer one moment and shorter the next, simply enjoy the sensa-tion, becoming aware of the stillpoint between the in-breath and the out-breath ... (*15 seconds*).

4 And now on every out-breath, count 'one'; and then 'two' and so on up to ten. Remember, count only on the out-breath. Once you reach ten, go back to one again. If you lose count or thoughts come crowding your mind (as they surely will), do not become irritated but gently push them aside and start counting again with one. Continue to count until you receive the signal to move out of your inner sanctuary. (*If directing this sequence, remain silent for ten minutes.*)

5 (*If directing this sequence, speak the following very softly so as not to startle the listener.*) Now it is time gradually to return to everyday awareness. Imagine that you are centred along a straight line running from the top of your head to your feet ... Feel composed and at peace ... (*five seconds*).

6 Open your eyes, shake out your limbs and have a good stretch from fingertips to toes. When you are ready, get up and resume your everyday activities with renewed energy and awareness.

RECITING A MANTRA OR MANTRAM

The use of a mantra (a single word or sound) or a mantram (a collection of words or sounds) can be used to aid concentration in meditation. It enhances the process by bringing a certain vibratory power into play. Although reciting a mantra may be labelled 'seriously weird' by some people, it is arguably the most potent tool of all for engendering a meditative state. Moreover, it is especially suitable for those prone to nervous tension, feelings of disorientation or emotional fragility. It is also a marvellous way to replenish psychic and physical energy. Nevertheless, it is important not to overuse the method, for it can lead to a state of dreamy self-hypnosis rather than clarity of mind.

A mantra or mantram may have no meaning at all, or if it does, the rhythm and quality of sound are more important. A classic example of a mantram is the Buddhist chant OM MANI PADME HUM (pronounced OM MANI PEYMAY HUNG) whose purpose is to lead the aspirant to the 'jewel in the lotus' or the spiritual self. It has a certain rolling rhythm which carries you along. This lessens the possibility of the chant becoming so boring that you give up too soon; that is, before it has time to exert its beneficial effects. The most popular mantra is the simple sound, AUM or OM. Although it has no meaning as such, according to Eastern mystics it harmonises the human soul with the cosmic 'sound of silence', or the subtle drone of the life-force itself. Alternatively, you may prefer to work with one of the following sounds:

AH	OM AH HUM
HUM	SHALOM
AH HUM	TAM LAM
OM AH	

The good thing about using sound as a focus for meditation is that there is no need to sit in a meditative position – unless, of course, you would prefer to do so. A mantra or mantram can be recited while you shower, relax in the bath, walk the dog or wash the dishes. It can be chanted (or spoken) fast or slow, either silently or aloud. However, it is always helpful to begin with an audible recitation of your chosen sound, until such time as your body and mind have become accustomed to its vibration. Thereafter, you will respond positively even to silent repetition of the syllables.

MEDITATING ON A SOUND

1 Whether you are sitting or standing, close your eyes for a few moments and breathe out with a sigh, allowing any physical and emotional tension to melt away.

2 If you are sitting in a meditative pose, you may prefer to chant or speak your chosen mantra or mantram with your eyes closed. Otherwise, with your eyes open, begin to repeat the sound over and over again, becoming immersed in its rhythm and resonance. If you begin to lose focus, try speeding up or slowing down. When

chanting, you could vary the quality of sound by intoning on a higher or deeper note, but not so high pitched or low as to strain your voice. It is important to discover the quality of sound that most naturally vibrates within your body and makes you feel good.

3 After 10 or 15 minutes of chanting, stop. Before getting on with anything else, allow yourself to rest for a few moments in the profound silence that often follows.

THE HEALING POWER OF MUSIC

A sense of rhythm and timing is inherent to human nature. Therefore, singing, chanting, listening to music or dancing can be a wonderful adjunct to any stress-reducing programme. It is especially helpful to those who find it hard to get in touch with their emotions. For music has the power to intensify feelings, evoke images and memories, and to transport us into a state of exhilaration, relaxation, sadness, joy or reverence, or simply to charm us through the delicacy of melody. Tribal dance rituals, frantic drumming and synchronised movement can lead to a state of trance or even ecstasy, while the drones and chants of Tibetan monks bring about a state of inner peace and unity.

Almost everyone has experienced the sensation of altered rate and rhythm of breathing – and the associated mood change –

triggered by music. But how does music exert such a powerful effect? In simple terms, music is perceived through the auditory apparatus in the ear from where it is channelled by means of neuro-chemical impulses to the limbic system of the brain. The limbic system is associated with our most primitive and subtle responses such as emotion, imagination, creativity and intuition. Even though the specific thoughts and feelings evoked vary in proportion and intensity to the ideas already in the mind, the *general* effects of music upon the mind/body can be predicted with a high degree of accuracy.

The human heart pulses at around 70 to 80 beats a minute. Therefore, any musical rhythm with a rate of less than 80 beats per minute is perceived as 'slow' and so tends to relax and soothe. On the other hand, music with more than 90 beats per minute is perceived as 'fast' and so exhilarates and excites. However, certain rhythmic patterns in music, especially the anapaestic beat of some forms of rock music, can have a devitalising effect on the human organism. An anapaestic rhythm consists of two short beats followed by one long or stressed beat – da: da: DA. According to music therapists, prolonged and repeated exposure to this particular rhythm can also result in a loss of symmetry between the two cerebral hemispheres of the brain, manifesting as stress in its many guises. Similarly, musical dissonance can have a detrimental effect on our well-being.

Nevertheless, it is interesting to note that a disliked piece of music will not always gain the same access to the central nervous system. In other words, we can impede its subtle influence. Even so, we may well experience overt irritation at having to listen to it! Clearly, such a response is a kind of psychic safety valve. It enables the listener to avoid the subliminal lure of potentially harmful rhythms. Indeed, for music to work its mood-altering magic, whether for good or ill, we need to be open to its influence, to perceive it as meaningful or enjoyable. The exception is the detrimental effects upon the nervous system of being forced to endure any persistent sound, such as loud music throbbing through the walls late at night.

Musical taste varies, of course, and this is largely due to cultural and social influences. However, many young people enjoy dissonant music, usually amplified to such an extent that it can be excruciatingly painful for those who are not fans to endure! It is little wonder that increasing numbers of people in their teens and early twenties are prematurely deaf. But why are young people attracted to harmful sounds? It seems that loudness combined with a frantic rhythm must excite them in an erotic way. Moreover, we all know that the moods of teenagers have a tendency to fluctuate wildly, swinging from elation to despair, from sudden adult insight to childish dependency and rebelliousness. Likewise, their favourite style of music is merely a reflection of physical and emotional turbulence. However, as the American psychologist Arlene Bronzaft warns, exposing people (especially adolescents and teenagers) to chronic noise 'amplifies aggression and tends to dampen healthful behaviour'.

Healthful Music

But what is healthful music? Since musical appreciation is a personal thing, it is difficult to suggest a list of healing music suitable for everyone. Nevertheless, it is interesting to note that certain tunes are popular the world over, for they have the power to stir the emotions in a specific way. The Irish song *Danny Boy* falls into this category. Say the words, 'O Danny boy the pipes, the pipes are calling, from glen to glen and down the mountainside' and nothing much happens. Add the famous haunting tune, and you may be moved to tears. Ironically, the songwriter was an Englishman, Fred Weatherly, whose clever Italianate placing of open vowels on high notes gave his words immediate appeal. Similarly, even without knowing the meaning of the words, the soaring melody of the black gospel hymn 'Amazing Grace' has the power to transport the Hindu to Nirvana, the Muslim to Allah and the atheist to Wonderland!

Many people are drawn to New Age or 'inner space' music whose aim is to enhance relaxation, meditation, visualisation and guided imagery. The signature of this kind of music is repeated cycles of gentle, undulating sounds. It is usually created by means of synthesisers in harmony with the sounds of traditional instruments like the piano, violin or flute, and sometimes the human voice. However, while most experts would agree that certain forms of music can enhance the relaxation response, some are sceptical about the whole concept of meditation music. Meditation is a state of listening inwardly, they remind us, and thus exterior sources of sound are barely perceived at all. None the less, because music can be an aid to relaxation, concentration and inner quietness, it can provide a meditative point of departure.

New Age music is available from some music shops, though it is more easily obtained by mail order from specialist suppliers (see Useful Addresses). These same outlets may also stock Eastern mystical music, liturgical chants, shamanic 'trance dance' compositions, alongside recordings of birdsong, the sound of the wind, rain, seashore, or the beautiful and unearthly songs of whales, dolphins and porpoises. Take your pick!

The Subtle Body

Much has been written on the relationship between specific sounds, whether made by the human voice, synthesisers or musical instruments, and the part of the body with which they resonate. For instance, sound therapists prescribe one sound to heal the liver, another for the stomach, another for a sore throat. They may also attempt to harmonise the vibrations of the subtle body.

The subtle body comprises the auric or electromagnetic field which surrounds and interpenetrates the physical form, and the chakras – a sanskrit term for the seven vortices of energy said to be located at specific points along the midline of the body – from the root chakra emanating from the pelvic area to the crown chakra at the top of the head (see the illustration opposite). It is also interesting to note that numerous 'lesser chakras' are said to emanate from other areas of the body, including the hands, knees and feet.

Each of the seven major chakras, however, corresponds to a different gland and governs specific parts of the physical body and areas of psychological and spiritual development. Even though the chakras are depicted in artwork as emanating from the front of the body, in fact, healers can perceive them (by touch and/or clairvoyance) both at the front and back.

What about the aura? Although healers describe the auric field differently (according to their own level of psychic perception), it is generally agreed that it is a rainbow-coloured emanation (some

KEY

Each chakra is associated with various bodily parts, physiological functions and states of mind:

CROWN: pineal, transcendence, spirituality

BROW: pituitary, intuition, intellect

THROAT: thyroid, self expression, creativity

HEART: thymus, love, compassion

SOLAR PLEXUS: pancreas, emotional energy, personal power

HARA: gonads, vitality, sexual expression

ROOT: adrenals, survival instinct

sensitives can see its hues) radiating half a metre or more around the physical form, more or less ovoid in shape. It shimmers and alters in colour depending on our thoughts, emotions and physical state. Although different healers assign different meanings to the individual colours perceived within the auric field, it is generally agreed that murky or grey hues indicate negative emotions or ill health; whereas bright or clear tones are a positive sign.

The part of the subtle body closest to the physical level, emanating about 2.5 cm from the body, is known as the etheric or vital body. It is from this level that the chakras radiate, acting as the main receivers and distributors of vital energy (prana) between the physical body and the auric field.

When the energies within the chakras are evenly balanced (for each has its own optimum resonant frequency) the body is in harmony with the mental, emotional and spiritual aspects of self. However, in a world of much stress and strain, the energies within the subtle body can become weakened, causing the chakras to vibrate at a slower or faster frequency and the colours within the auric field to appear less vibrant. Dysfunction within the subtle body may manifest on the physical level as some form of illness – be it a cold or flu, or something much more serious. At the emotional level we might feel gloomy or experience a chronic lack of interest in life, or there may be over-sensitivity and anger towards people or things. Mentally, we may suffer from vagueness of thought or lack insight into everyday problems.

However, since the chakras are essentially spheres of energy or vibration, they can be brought into harmony by the use of certain sounds and rhythms. When the chakras are vibrated in a specific way, subtle energy starts to move. In so doing, we experience a wonderful release of physical and emotional tension and enhanced vitality (techniques for achieving this are given in Voice Workshop and Dance of the Soul).

Incidentally, British scientist Harry Oldfield, inventor of a high-tech scanning device utilising electrically-charged crystals, has confirmed the existence of subtle energy-centres which coincide exactly with the seven major chakras. Moreover, there is also a high voltage photographic technique called bio-feedback imaging which is used to capture on film the human aura in all its technicolour glory. The camera, which imposes the auric field on to polaroid film, has been used in the US since the early 1980s.

Voice Workshop

Although it may seem paradoxical, different sound therapists apparently use different sounds to heal the same problem. How can this be? As the American pianist and musicologist Dr Steven Halpern explains, 'Sound is a carrier wave of consciousness'. This means that when a healer creates a sound with conscious intent and awareness it becomes a transformative and therapeutic tool. For thought itself is energy or vibration, and therefore has the ability to interact with the sound tool. Indeed, as every healer knows, the 'mind over matter' phenomenon is an essential part of the healing process.

Nevertheless, there are a few sounds which resonate with specific parts of the body (and perhaps also with the related chakras) without the power of intent. For example, if you put the palm of your hand on your chest and chant 'Ah' you feel the vibration mainly in your sternum or breast bone. Chant 'Oo' and the strongest resonance will be felt in the throat and lower part of the face. Now put your hand on the crown of your head and chant 'Mm' and you will feel the vibration in your skull.

You may also enjoy experimenting with the following voice exercise, Wind Song, which combines the power of the breath with sound to vibrate different parts of the body and skull. And, in so doing, it uplifts the spirits and brings about inner peace.

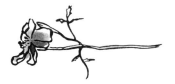

WIND SONG

1 Sit comfortably in any of the meditative positions recommended earlier. Close your eyes and breathe out with a deep sigh, allowing any tension to melt away.

2 Breathe in slowly through your nose. As you exhale, loosly purse your lips and make the sound 'Whoo', holding on to the note for as long as you can. If done correctly, the sound should be airy and ethereal, like the breeze moving through hollow reeds.

3 While making the sound, place the palm of your hand over your sternum, abdomen, and so forth, in correspondence with the location of each chakra. This will enable you to discover the pitch which resonates most powerfully in each of these places. Then begin to move the pitch upwards to the crown of your head, and then down again, but without straining the voice. There is no scale, just a slurred tone moving gently up and down.

4 As you continue to vibrate different parts of your body and skull you may notice that certain thoughts or emotions appear in response to certain tones. If this is the case, concentrate on the tones that make you feel best. Continue with the exercise for about five or ten minutes. Before getting on with anything else, rest for a few moments in the tranquillity that often follows.

DANCE OF THE SOUL

Dance, especially if it is undirected and free, is one of the most powerful ways to get in touch with our feelings and counter stress. As well as being a superb physical and emotional release, it encourages spontaneity and the confidence to be true to ourselves and others. However, many people feel awkward about expressing themselves in such an uninhibited way. Yet they may be less reluctant to take up some form of structured movement such as ballroom dancing, tap, country dancing or aerobic-type dance, rather than reveal themselves through their own soul dance. Not that there is anything intrinsically wrong with formalised movement. On the contrary, it can be most enjoyable and revitalising. None the less, stylised movement carries with it an element of competitiveness. This acts to curb free expression, thus hindering the flow of a specific kind of energy essential to the process of true healing.

When we surrender to the spirit of free dance we begin to feel at ease with the lack of external structure. Thus we develop new ways of relating to ourselves, to other people and the world about us. Moreover, free expressive dance can release a great deal of energy hitherto locked up in muscular tension and patterned ways of thinking. As a result, we experience a wonderful sensation of lightness and well-being.

Ideally, soul dance is best performed outdoors with a group of like-minded friends, say, on the seashore, in a forest glade, green meadow or perhaps around a bonfire in the garden. However, this is not always possible for all manner of reasons, not least through lack of privacy. Indeed, the neighbours (or passers-by) may think you have gone mad! Luckily, it can also be performed indoors – by yourself or with a friend or two.

You may wish to vaporise any of the following energising essential oils (or a blend of two or three) to enhance the experience. (*Instructions for vaporising essential oils are to be found on page 56.*)

SUGGESTED ESSENTIAL OILS

basil
bergamot
coriander
elemi
grapefruit
juniper berry

lavender
lemon
lemongrass
palmarosa
pine
rosemary

Soul Dance and the Chakras

The purpose of soul dance is to encourage expression of at least two sides of our nature – the flowing aquatic and the earthy primitive. The flowing part of the dance resonates mainly with the energies of the heart chakra and those above it; whereas the strong pulse of the earthy dance finds resonance with the solar plexus chakra and those below it (refer back to the illustration on page 31). In reality, however, none of the chakras exists in isolation. When we influence the vibration of one, we influence to a degree the energy of an adjacent chakra, and so a wave of energy spreads throughout. None the less, by expressing ourselves through both aspects of the dance, and therefore connecting strongly with each chakra, we bring the entire system into a state of harmonious vibration.

HOW TO SOUL DANCE

Wear loose, comfortable clothing and remove your shoes. If the surface does not permit you to go barefoot, put on some light protective footwear.

For the flowing dance you will need music without a clear rhythmical beat – perhaps a classical piece such as Debussy's *Clair de Lune*, or a New Age composition with an oceanic or watery mood. For the wild and abandoned dance, the ideal rhythm would be fast shamanic drumming. Tapes and CDs of this style of music are available from specialist outlets (see Useful Addresses). Or if you know someone who could provide live sound on a deep-toned traditional drum, such as the Irish bodhran, this would be perfect. Alternatively, any music with a strong rhythmic pulse of around 90 beats per minute would be fine.

►

The duration of each dance session can be anything from 20 to 90 minutes, depending on your stamina. However, should you 'lose yourself' in the dance, then you will become oblivious to both the passing of time and the amount of energy expended. This is much more likely to occur when dancing with others rather than by yourself for the energies of everyone within a harmonious group become as one. And the energy of the whole becomes far greater than the sum of its separate parts.

Begin with the flowing music. To enable you to feel the music inside your body, it can be helpful to dance with your eyes closed. Move with the sounds; swirl around the dance area, allowing your body to express itself in whatever way it wants to. Even with your eyes closed, you will still be aware of other dancers in your sphere (if you have chosen to dance with others) and will not necessarily collide with them. But even if you do, and it makes you laugh, this is part of the joy of the dance. When the music has finished, immediately put on the next piece – and move ecstatically. This time you may even feel the urge to express your emotions by exhaling forcibly with a 'Ha' sound, or perhaps by whooping – or whatever demands to be heard. Forget your inhibitions, voice it – and enjoy it!

2 Emotion and Meaning

*A*CCORDING to Mr Spock. the Vulcan alien in *Star Trek*, humans squander inordinate amounts of energy reacting emotionally to things when a more logical and rational outlook would be far more productive. While a totally objective approach may be fine for Vulcans, as far as we humans are concerned, emotions add colour, richness and meaning to our lives. Just like ocean undercurrents, they are the energising forces which direct and sustain behaviour. Moreover, it is our capacity to have feelings as well as to think and reason which defines us as a species.

WHAT IS EMOTION?

But what exactly is emotion? One widely held view is that something happens which produces in us a subjective feeling and, as a result of this, certain bodily and/or behavioural changes occur. Well-known physiological changes involving the nervous system and the endocrine system result in such sensations as 'gooseflesh', butterflies in the stomach, sweating, blushing, and a pounding heart. Behaviours and facial expressions associated with such emotions include crying, smiling, frowning, running away or perhaps being frozen on the spot. However, there are those psychologists who have turned this theory on its head, for they postulate that our emotional experience is the *result* not the cause, of perceived bodily changes. For example, we experience grief because we cry, anger because we strike or fear because we tremble.

While this may seem ludicrous as a generalised theory, there are times when an emotion really is experienced as a result of feedback from the bodily processes. For instance, should you eat an overly rich meal and suffer indigestion as a consequence, no doubt you will also feel irritable. Similarly, hidden food allergies can trigger discomfiting thoughts. Conversely, there are those foods which contribute to a sense of well-being (see Chapter 3). To take a completely different example, should you slip when coming down the stairs, your automatic reaction is to grab for the banisters. Only afterwards do you become aware of feeling frightened (and a little shaken).

A more subtle illustration of this process is when we feel an inexplicable uneasiness in the presence of a certain person, place or thing. Later, we may learn that the person who made us feel 'heavy and grey', even without speaking to us, has a history of depressive illness, the landscape that sent shivers up our spine was formerly the site of a bloody battle; and the pair of old boots in the hallway which caused our heart to move with grief belonged to someone who recently died in an horrific road accident.

If the truth be known, almost everyone can recall some such incident – be it positive, mediocre or distressing – whereby the intuitive responses proved to be uncannily accurate. Sometimes the mind/body knows no bounds, as in the case of the person who suddenly 'knows' that a loved one has just died, albeit many thousands of miles away.

But, in order to answer the question 'What is emotion?', it would seem that a multi-factorial model would be far more feasible than either one of the aforementioned theories. In other words, while it is true that we react emotionally to bodily feedback, we are also capable of initiating emotion – irrespective of our bodily state. In so doing, our emotions can exert a powerful influence over our immune responses and overall state of health.

Indeed, every thought, emotion and action is reflected by a cascade of biochemical responses throughout the whole organism. The most important of these are certain brain hormones called neuro-transmitters and neuro-peptides. Receptors for these chemicals are to be found all over the body, notably the skin and on cells in the immune system called monocytes. These 'intelligent' blood cells circulate freely throughout the body, apparently send-

ing and receiving messages just as diverse as those in the central nervous system. This means that if, when we are happy, depressed, angry, in love or whatever, we produce brain chemicals in various parts of the body, then those parts must also be happy, depressed, angry or in love. Moreover (as if this were not astonishing enough), insulin, a hormone always associated with the pancreas, is now known to be produced in the brain as well, just as brain chemicals such as transferon and CCK are produced in the stomach. Without doubt, the interrelated *mindbody* is a reality.

THE BACH FLOWER REMEDIES

The Bach flower remedy system of healing was developed by the British physician Dr Edward Bach in the 1930s. The remedies are prepared from the non-poisonous flowers of certain trees, plants and shrubs (the majority of which are found growing in the British Isles); they are benign in their action, non-addictive and can be taken by people of all ages. The remedies help us transmute negative feelings such as anger, jealousy and fear into optimism and joy.

Flower therapy is a wonderful adjunct to any de-stressing programme and can even bring benefit to those who are trying to wean themselves off tranquillisers, anti-depressants and other mood-altering drugs. But instead of masking reality, they help us to connect with our own inner strength, and thus we become better enabled to weather the storms of life.

How Do the Remedies Work?

The flower remedies can be used to support any other form of healing, be it counselling, acupuncture, homoeopathy, herbal medicine, aromatherapy, even conventional treatment. They work on the emotional/spiritual level, so they will not interfere with any other means of healing the body. Those therapists who employ the Bach flower remedies in their work (including a growing number of orthodox medical practitioners) would agree that they enhance other forms of treatment. In my own experience as an aromatherapist, the flower remedies help release ingrained fear and tension which can manifest as cold, painful or over-sensitive areas in the body – the feet, solar plexus, shoulders or buttocks, for example. The remedies appear to hasten the healing process, especially in those who find it extremely difficult to let go.

Flower remedies could be likened to homoeopathic medicines, for they are so highly diluted that not a single molecule of the original medicinal substance remains in the brandy carrier. Rather, the liquid emanates the energy pattern or blueprint of the original plant material. (Incidentally, the differing energy patterns of individual flower remedies can be captured by high voltage equipment such as Kirlian photography.) Yet if the correct remedy (or composite of remedies) is chosen, the effect upon the mind and emotions can be pronounced.

In common with other vibrational methods of healing, such as colour therapy, crystal healing and spiritual healing, the remedies' mode of action is extremely difficult to explain in everyday terms. We might say that ordinary herbal medicines (those which are pharmacologically active) vibrate at the same frequency to that of the physical body; whereas the flower remedies find resonance with the faster frequencies of the emotional/spiritual aspect of our being.

Many therapists working with these remedies believe that the healing effect is triggered in the human energy field or aura (see pages 30–1) which surrounds and interpenetrates the physical aspect. From this field, which is essentially a thought form, the healing effect of the remedies filters 'inwards', as it were, to the physical level. In contrast, material medicines such as herbs and conventional drugs move 'outwards' from the physical level, eventually affecting the auric field.

Researchers such as Thrity Engineer, a psychotherapist who lives and works in London, use bio-feedback imaging to monitor the effects of the Himalayan flower essences (similar to the Bach remedies) upon the human aura. It has been found that within minutes of taking a carefully chosen flower essence, the colours within the auric field become brighter and clearer, indicating a state of increased vitality and emotional equilibrium.

Buying the Remedies

The modestly priced Bach flower remedies come in little dark-glass dropper bottles labelled 'Stock Concentrate'. They can be obtained from many health shops, a few chemists or by mail order. The Stock Concentrates will keep indefinitely if stored in a cool, dark place. Once diluted in water, however, the prescription should be kept cool (in the fridge) and used up within four weeks.

Dosages and Methods of Use

Since we are dealing with the *energy* of the plant, rather than its material properties, exact quantities are not at all crucial; more important is the frequency of the dose. Although the remedy can be taken neat, say, two to four drops as required, when taking more than one remedy it is far more practicable to make up a treatment bottle. The usual recommended quantity is two drops of each Stock Concentrate added to a 30 ml dropper medicine bottle (available from most chemists), three-quarters filled with bottled water (not tap water as this soon develops mould) and topped up with brandy, vodka or cider vinegar as a preservative. Having prepared the treatment bottle (which should be enough for three to four weeks) the usual dosage is four drops directly on the tongue, three or four times daily. However, the most important times for taking the remedy are upon rising and at bedtime.

Rescue remedy

When taking the five-flower composite known as Rescue Remedy (comprising: Star of Bethlehem, Rock Rose, Impatiens, Cherry Plum and Clematis), Dr Bach advocated taking four drops of the neat remedy directly on the tongue as required. As its name implies, it is the first-aid remedy for all emergency situations – where there is panic, shock, hysteria or mental numbness. Although the remedy cannot replace medical attention, it can alleviate much distress while the person awaits the arrival of medical aid, thus enabling the mindbody's healing processes to commence without delay. It is also a good addition to the first-aid box.

Duration of Treatment

There are no hard and fast rules about the length of time the remedies should be continued. Treatment is always geared towards
individual needs. For acute conditions such as the effects of bad
news (Rescue Remedy, Star of Bethlehem), that 'Monday morning
feeling' (Hornbeam) or exam nerves (Mimulus, Larch), for example, take the drops as often as needed. This could be every 15 minutes or so until you feel better. It is common to feel some relief
almost immediately, but more especially after an hour or so.

When dealing with deeply ingrained emotional disharmony – a
domineering and inflexible personality (Vine, Beech), for example,
or the lingering effects of some past trauma (Star of Bethlehem) –
the healing process may take many months. As each layer within
the psyche begins to peel away like the many layers of an onion,
different emotions will emerge, feelings you may have held in
check for many years. Note any negative change (of course, positive
feelings will also surface) and alter the prescription accordingly.

An indication of improvement is when you begin to feel better
physically and emotionally, and when family and friends notice the
difference – but more especially when you forget to take the remedies! This means you are becoming less self-interested and beginning to flow outwards to others and the world about you.

Finding the Right Remedy

On first acquaintance with the flower remedy descriptions (see the
Flower Remedy Repertory below), you may feel you need all of
them! Bach made a point of testing a composite of all 38 remedies,
but was not satisfied with the result. He found that the vibration
of one correctly chosen flower had a deeper and more profound
effect than several. However, many people may temporarily
require a composite of between three and six flowers.

The best way to begin is to write down the remedies you feel
you need, then look at each one more closely in order to ascertain
the most pressing areas of imbalance. Cross off those remedies
which you feel could be helpful at a later date, or perhaps dis-
pensed with altogether. This enables you to focus on key issues
and to begin to open to the possibility of change.

BACH FLOWER REMEDY REPERTORY

The following 38 concise profiles are offered as a prompt to enable you to begin prescribing for yourself. However, it is essential to be totally honest with yourself – no easy task. Therefore, you may find it helpful to ask someone else (a person who knows you well) to help you choose the remedies – though be prepared for a few home truths! For more detailed information about every aspect of flower therapy, including the techniques of flower therapy counselling, see Suggested Reading.

	Pattern of imbalance	Positive potential		Pattern of imbalance	Positive potential
Agrimony	Mental torture concealed behind a happy-go-lucky facade.	The ability truly to laugh at life because personal problems are viewed from a more balanced perspective.	**Centaury**	Lacks willpower to refuse the demands of others, the 'doormat' personality; suppresses own needs to keep the peace and to gain favour in the eyes of another.	To know when to give and when to withhold; the ability to relate with others while preserving one's own identity.
Aspen	Inexplicable fears stemming from the psyche; nightmares; fear of some impending evil; delusions.	Fearlessness in the knowledge that one's Guardian is the universal power of love.	**Cerato**	Annoys others by constantly asking their advice; imitative; lacks concentration; appears foolish at times; saps others.	Trusts own inner voice; gains self-confidence.
Beech	Intolerant, hypercritical and arrogant; lacks empathy and therefore has few friends; perfectionist or unrealistic expectations of others.	Tolerance and understanding of the difficulties of others; the ability to see good in people.	**Cherry Plum**	Fear of losing one's sanity; uncontrolled outbreaks of temper; fear of harming self or others; nervous breakdown; violent temperament through fear.	Balance and equanimity despite extreme anguish; a feeling of protection.

	Pattern of imbalance	Positive potential		Pattern of imbalance	Positive potential
Chestnut Bud	Failure to learn by experience; that 'Oh no, not again!' feeling; lacks observation; thoughts more often in the future rather than the present.	The ability to keep the attention in the present; to gain knowledge and wisdom from every experience.	**Crab Apple**	A feeling of being unclean; self-disgust; overemphasis on trivial detail; houseproud; fussy; anxious; obsessed with imperfection; disgusted by bodily functions such as breastfeeding, going to the toilet or illness; may have a skin complaint.	The wisdom to see things in their proper perspective; self respect; acceptance of the physical body.
Chicory	Possessive of people and things; demands sympathy, love and affection; may use emotional blackmail; fears losing friends; self-centred; saps others; strong willed; may be houseproud.	Selfless love given freely; inner security and wisdom.	**Elm**	Temporary feelings of inadequacy, even though fulfilling one's true mission in life. (Compare **Hornbeam**, whose fatigue is through dislike of their work, and **Olive**, who is worn out by continued stress eg such as illness or an unhappiness. Elm types love their work, but need to recharge their battteries from time to time.)	The ability to see problems in their proper perspective; an inner conviction that help will always come at the right moment.
Clematis	A day-dreamer, with thoughts often far away in the future; lacks ambition; impractical; needs a great deal of sleep; may feign illness to escape from life; is sapped by others. Clematis is also the remedy for any bemused state of mind.	To take a lively interest in things because the purpose of life can be fully appreciated.			

	Pattern of imbalance	Positive potential		Pattern of imbalance	Positive potential
Gentian	Depressed through setback; easily discouraged; a 'doubting Thomas' attitude.	Perseverance; the faith of a positive sceptic – one who sees difficulties, but does not fall into a deep gloom over them.	**Holly**	Feeling cut off from love; envy, jealousy, anger, hatred; may have a violent temperament; suspicious; saps others.	To feel loved and able to love others; the ability to give without thought of recompense; to rejoice in the good fortune of others.
Gorse	Hopelessness and despair, may be chronically ill and feels nothing more can be done, yet *can* be persuaded to try again, albeit half-heartedly. (Compare with the **Wild Rose** type who is even more apathetic and is unable to muster the enthusiasm to try again, even to please their loved ones.)	The knowledge that all difficulties will be overcome in the end; glimpsing the light at the end of the tunnel.	**Honey-suckle**	Nostalgic; lives in the past; suffers deep regret; homesick; fears the ageing process; perhaps obsessed with past life theory to the detriment of the present life; often sad; saps others.	The ability to retain the lessons taught by past experiences, but not to cling to memories at the expense of the present.
Heather	Self-centred, saps others with non-stop talking, may give graphic accounts of all their illnesses; fears being alone; poor listener; mentally congested; childish; weeps easily.	Great empathy as a result of having suffered; a good listener; emotionally secure.	**Hornbeam**	Tiredness, weariness; that 'Monday morning' feeling; boredom or laziness, especially in connection with one's daily duties.	A renewed interest in life; energy and involvement in daily tasks.

	Pattern of imbalance	Positive potential		Pattern of imbalance	Positive potential
Impatiens	Impatient and irritable; desires to work alone at own swift pace; over-works; has high ideals so finds fault with others; quick in mind and body, often resulting in nervous tension and muscular pain; sometimes angry or violent.	Great empathy, patience and tolerance, especially towards the shortcomings of others. The ability to relax.	**Mustard**	Fluctuating cycles of black depression, without an obvious cause.	Inner serenity; the ability to transmute melancholia into joy and peace.
			Oak	Despondency as a result of obstinate, relentless effort against all odds; life viewed as uphill struggle; refuses to give in to illness; may suffer nervous breakdown or collapse.	Balanced strength in adversity; accepting one's limits and therefore knowing when to surrender.
Larch	Lacks confidence, expects failure so rarely bothers to try; may feign illness to avoid responsibility; weak-willed.	The courage to plunge into life and to fulfil one's true potential. Balanced self-confidence.	**Olive**	Complete mental and physical exhaustion. (Compare with **Hornbeam**, whose weariness is more of the mind, that 'I can't be bothered going to work today' feeling. The **Olive** exhaustion is the result of over-exertion during childbirth, for example, or a long illness.)	Peace of mind, revitalisation; a renewed interest in life.
Mimulus	Fear of *known* things such as flying, animals, water, public speaking, going to the dentist, and so forth. (Compare with **Aspen**, whose fears are less tangible.)	The quiet courage to face trials and difficulties; becoming understanding and supportive of others in a similar situation. To overcome specific fears.			

	Pattern of imbalance	Positive potential		Pattern of imbalance	Positive potential
Pine	Self-reproach; guilt, blaming self for the wrongdoings of others.	Self-acceptance; self-forgiveness; the ability to let go of the past; to take responsibility with a fair and and balanced attitude.	**Rock Water** *(This is not a plant, but potentised spring water)*	Too rigid self-discipline; repression and self-denial; fixed ideas and opinions combined with perfectionism, intolerant, but not openly critical of others, a tendency towards fanaticism. May help those suffering from eating disorders.	Open-minded idealism; radiating joy and peace, thus a natural example to others; ability to let go and enjoy!
Red Chestnut	Fear and excessive concern for the welfare of others; always imagines the worst; is extremely distressed by reports of war, famine or other disasters.	The ability to send out thoughts of safety, health and courage to those who need them; to keep a cool head in emergencies.			
Rock Rose	An extremely acute state of fear, terror or panic – at the site of an horrific accident, for example. May be helpful for those who suffer panic attacks or recurrent nightmares (see also **Rescue Remedy**, page 41).	Great courage in the face of adversity.	**Scleranthus**	Suffers from mood swings and procrastination; tends to be unrealiable; lacks concentration; has little confidence; unstable; may suffer nervous breakdown or collapse; lacks poise; restless; may have violent temperament.	The ability to make a decision quickly and to act promptly; to maintain poise and balance whatever the circumstances.

	Pattern of imbalance	Positive potential		Pattern of imbalance	Positive potential
Star of Bethlehem	Shock or trauma, either recent or from a past experience; grief; emotional numbness. This remedy can often be the catalyst required if shock or truama has been sustained and can be identified as the cause of the present distress, which can manifest as long-term guilt, anxiety or anger, or perhaps in the guise of some physical complaint.	A neutralisation of the effect of shock or trauma, whether immediate or delayed.	**Vervain**	Strain and tension as a result of over-enthusiasm; a tendency to hyperactivity; obsessive missionary zeal; interference in the affairs of others; talkative; a martyr to the cause; may suffer nervous breakdown or collapse.	The realisation that others have the right to their opinions; the wisdom to change one's mind as a result of discussion and debate; the ability to relax.
			Vine	A domineering and inflexible personality; intolerant; lacks sympathy; violent temperament.	The attainment of wisdom and compassion within leadership; the ability to guide rather than to dominate.
Sweet Chestnut	Extreme mental anguish, perhaps triggered by some life-shattering event; the utmost limits of endurance; paroxysms of grief; feeling utterly alone; unable even to pray.	Hope returns; the end of torment is at last within reach. Personal experiences of the true meaning of life.	**Walnut**	Difficulties adjusting to change of any nature; may be held back or misguided by others; feels 'stuck' in present situation. (The remedy can also be used for easing the transitions of puberty, pregnancy and the menopause.)	Freedom from limiting circumstances; the courage to carry through one's ideals and ambitions despite adverse circumstances, damning comments and ridicule.

	Pattern of imbalance	Positive potential		Pattern of imbalance	Positive potential
Water Violet	Proud and aloof; disdainful of social relationships; suffers in silence; physical rigidity; radiates superiority.	Although remaining serene and self-contained, has the wisdom and sympathy to put own capabilities to the service of others.	**Wild Rose**	Apathy and resignation; 'I'll have to live with it' attitude; neither happy nor unhappy; emotionally 'flat'.	A renewed interest in life and, with the return of one's vitality, the enrichment and enjoyment of friendship.
White Chestnut	Persistent worrying thoughts and mental arguments; may suffer from insomnia; lacks observation; worried.	Peace of mind and a solution to problems.	**Willow**	Bitter and resentful – 'poor me' attitude; selfish; enjoys arguments; blames others; grumpy and morose; may simulate illness to obtain pity; irritable and sulky.	Optimism and a sense of humour; the ability to accept responsibility for one's own life and health, and to see things in their true perspective
Wild Oat	Dissatisfaction because one's true vocation has not been found; a 'Jack of all trades, master of none'.	The realisation of one's true vocation.			

Realistic Expectations of the Remedies

The flower remedies cannot be compared with conventional mood-elevating drugs which can often engender a state alien to our own personality. As Edward Bach himself said: 'The remedies help us to feel ourselves again, at a point where we ceased to be quite ourselves'. And to feel ourselves again is a perfectly natural state of being, a state which can be easily overlooked if our expectations are unrealistic. So do not expect to feel 'high' or in any way unusual, but simply become open and receptive to the remedies' ability to engender greater clarity in your life.

It should be mentioned, however, that during the first weeks of flower therapy you may feel a temporary deepening of emotional disharmony. If this is the case rest assured that any aggravation will only last a few days. It is a positive sign that the correct remedy has been chosen and that earlier blockages are working their way to the surface and out through your system. It is often said that 'you cannot get out what is not already there', so such a reaction is not a side-effect, as in drug therapy, but an indication that your own mind/body is correcting itself, the flower remedies acting as a catalyst in the process.

OTHER WAYS TO DISCHARGE PENT-UP EMOTION

It is important to emphasise that flower therapy is not about putting on a brave face and fighting back the tears. This will only succeed in creating even more stress, tension and conflict – just as tensing up against physical pain succeeds in causing greater pain. True, wearing some kind of mask is often seen as an essential part of civilised behaviour. As a long-term option, however, it can lead to chronic negativity that festers beneath the surface and becomes the root cause of all manner of physical ailments. Therefore, it is important that we find a way to express negativity in order to release it. Indeed, the flower remedies often enable us to confront feelings which may have been held in check for many years. However, rather than taking it out on the family, friends or colleagues, there are other ways of harmlessly discharging pent-up emotion.

Safely Blow a Fuse!

Whenever a powerful emotion such as fear or anger begins to well up – especially if the feeling has become habitual – if possible, find an isolated spot such as the middle of a field, a hilltop, or perhaps beside a fast-flowing river or stream. Then take a deep breath and scream or shout with all your might, releasing the bottled-up anger, frustration, jealousy, hatred, or whatever it might be. If isolation is impossible (as is often the case), the next best option is to scream or shout into a deep pillow or cushion to muffle the sound, then beat the hell out of it with your fists or a cricket bat! To add fire to the experience, you may find it easier to let off steam while listening to some form of aggressive music, whether it be classical or rock. Indeed, every kind of music has its place in the holistic scheme of things!

Unfortunately, people who need to let loose in this manner are often too reserved to do so – rationalising their fear by calling the exercise childish, undignified or simply useless. A few may consider such release harmful, perhaps leading to extreme loss of self-control, or even of one's sanity. If this echoes your own feelings about releasing powerful emotion, instead of turning the aggression inwards, learn to harness it, using its dynamism to give more steam to any project or activity.

When you are actually feeling some form of aggression, focus inwards and really feel its vigour and the effect it has on your body. Now realise that these feelings are at your disposal: know that, although they can hurt, they can also become the propelling force for any activity you may have chosen. It may be a blitz on the housework, a long overdue letter of complaint to some authority – or why not start that novel?

If the target of your wrath is someone you know personally, write a venomous letter to that person, but do not send it. Instead, ritualistically destroy it, perhaps by burning it or tearing it into many pieces before scattering the fragments to the four winds. You will probably feel a great deal better for having vented your wrath, and relieved that there were no embarrassing repercussions. On the other hand, having expressed your true feelings, it may be appropriate to send a more tactful and socially acceptable version of the letter, but one still stating your position on an issue.

Cry Buckets

Although it may at first seem like masochism, if you are depressed, but cannot cry, listen to any form of music that triggers sad memories. Or you may prefer to watch a tragic film or television drama; read a heart-rending novel; or look at old photographs and wallow in nostalgia. It also helps to have an understanding friend or loved one with whom to confide. Talking about cares and woes with an emphatic person can often make them a little easier to bear – especially if that person has survived a similar crisis.

However, if you really cannot let go and the wounds continue to fester, especially if the distress is deep-rooted or has lingered for many years, professional counselling may be the answer. A skilful counsellor or therapist will help you to work through the feelings in a safe environment. Your doctor may be able to recommend a reputable and fully accredited person in your area.

Have a Good Belly Laugh

Having a laugh can sometimes seem inappropriate in a troubled world. However, by encouraging the mind/body to produce feel-good neuro-hormones, laughter can be a powerful tool for changing our perspective on seemingly frightening or worrying situations. So whenever the opportunity presents itself, get together with a group of jovial friends and laugh the night (or day) away. Alternatively, watch a hilarious film, play or television drama, or read a funny book.

Interestingly, psychologists tell us that those who are 'ultra-conforming' to a higher degree than society expects of them, commonly suffer from chronic anxiety or depression. On the contrary, non-conformists tend to live longer and seldom get seriously depressed. The secret, we are told, is to be found in laughter, especially that which takes the form of a mischievous sense of fun. So next time the going gets too serious, step back for a moment and have a good belly laugh at yourself and society – and glory in your individuality!

On Cultivating Self-Love

Although a hackneyed concept in therapy circles, it is important to mention that before we can truly love another, we must first love ourselves. We might 'need' someone, cling to them, pity them, idolise them – but only when our own cup is full to the brim can it overflow to others. Indeed, positive self-esteem is the foundation for enjoying life and creating healthy relationships.

Yet many people believe that they would love themselves if only someone would love them first. Does this reflect your own belief system? The truth is, you are the principal source of your own happiness. So, rather than looking outside of yourself for the right partner (or social circle) you must first learn to regard yourself as a person worthy of love. However, the fostering of self-love is not about being narcissistic and disregarding of others. Rather, it means feeling the same love and respect for yourself that you would feel for a good friend.

One way to begin cultivating self-love is to give to yourself the same time, space and pampering you might give a lover. For instance, luxuriate in an aromatic bath, then lovingly massage your body with fragrant oils (see Chapter 3). If you live alone, make a habit (at least once a week) of preparing an exquisite meal for yourself and eating it in style. Buy yourself a small gift every so often – a few flowers, an appealing picture card, an exotic fruit and so on.

Although you cannot learn to love yourself overnight, these small steps help foster a sense of well-being and self-worth. But even if feelings of self-doubt continue to linger in the unconscious mind, just going through the motions is often enough to activate the healing process. If you carry out self-nurturing activities often enough, eventually your unconscious mind will register the message that you are a person deserving of love and respect, and then others will begin to see you in the same light. And if it is a loving sexual relationship that you desire, having achieved a state of positive self-esteem, the chances are that you will attract into your life a person with whom you can share a deep and lasting relationship. Here's wishing you joy!

HEALING AROMAS

Another way to reduce stress and nurture the emotions is through the art of fragrant alchemy – the creation of mood-enhancing room scents.

It is important to use pure essences distilled from aromatic plants, for synthetic fragrance oils (usually labelled 'pot pourri refresher oil' or 'perfume oil') are much more likely to trigger allergic reactions like sneezing and wheezing. A natural, highly concentrated essence will be labelled 'pure essential oil'. However, you may come across a product labelled 'aromatherapy oil'. This is is certain to be a mixture of pure essential oil diluted in a base oil like sweet almond, grapeseed or jojoba. While such blends are fine for aromatherapy massage, the aroma is not powerful enough for perfuming rooms.

Genuine, undiluted essential oils (as used in aromatherapy) are widely available from health shops, or they can be purchased by mail order from specialist suppliers (see Useful Addresses). But before we get on to the basics of environmental perfumery, let us take a brief survey of the sense of smell and its influence upon the emotions.

The Sense of Smell

The area of the brain concerned with smell (the olfactory bulb) is an aspect of the mysterious limbic system. Although largely uncharted territory, the limbic system is concerned with our instinctive drives: emotion, intuition, memory, creativity, hunger, sleep patterns, sex drive and probably much more. The olfactory bulb also connects with the hypothalamus, a very important structure which controls the entire endocrine (hormonal) system by influencing the 'master gland' itself – the pituitary. Therefore, the influence of aroma upon the mind/body is potentially far reaching.

To take just one simple and well-known example: the delicious aroma of your favourite food will stimulate your appetite by making your mouth water and at the same time causing the digestive juices in the stomach to flow. If it is a special festive dish, you will more than likely have many joyful memories to savour as well.

A great deal of scientific research into the psychotherapeutic effects of aromatic plant essences (essential oils) has been carried out in recent years using electroencephalogram (EEG) instruments which record electrical activity of the brain and skin. Without doubt, certain aromas exert a relaxing effect on the central nervous system and others have a stimulating effect, whereas a few are apparently capable of engendering relaxation or mental alertness depending upon the state of the individual (refer to the Psychotherapeutic Aromas chart on page 57). At the same time, if an aroma is perceived as pleasant, odour stimuli in the limbic system cause a release of encephalins and endorphins, which help to reduce pain and create feelings of well-being. A disliked aroma, on the other hand, will not gain the same access, hence the importance of selecting essential oils according to your aroma preference.

Aromatic Harmony

Aromatherapists rarely use single essences, but prefer to blend two, three or more oils to create a fragrant compound. A carefully composed blend often works better aesthetically than a single essence. However, there is no reason why you should not use a single essence if the aroma appeals to your senses. Interestingly, we tend to be attracted to the oils that we need at a given time, and these usually mirror our emotional state. For example, when we feel nervy and restless, we tend to be attracted to light-hearted, highly volatile scents which are just as quick tempered as we are. Such essences give a swift embrace before disappearing into the ether – essences such as basil, bergamot, lemongrass, lavender, geranium and petitgrain. At other times, when we are feeling less fragile, we may prefer the lingering, mellow scents of such essences as cedarwood, frankincense, sandalwood, rose or ylang ylang.

When blending essential oils for the first time, it is helpful to remember that 'families' of essences tend to harmonise; for example, **herbs** (clary sage, lavender, marjoram, peppermint, rosemary), **citrus** (bergamot, lemon, orange, lime, mandarin), **flowers** (rose, ylang ylang, jasmine, neroli), **spices** (coriander, cinnamon, cloves, ginger, cardomom), **resins** (frankincense, galbanum, elemi), **woods** (sandalwood, cedarwood), **grasses** (vetiver, lemongrass, palmarosa). Other compatible aromas are spices and citrus with a hint of floral (coriander, bergamot, rose). Woods and resins are a good match too: cedarwood and frankincense is a classic. Another popular harmony is woods and flowers: rose and sandalwood being perfect marriage partners.

Of course, there are many other possibilities (as the blends suggested in this chapter and elsewhere would suggest). The more familiar you become with essential oils, the easier it is to choose what is best for you. Simply allow your developing sense of smell to lead you where it may; and you will discover that there is always an aromatic blend to suit every nuance of mood.

Essential Equipment

The most effective way to perfume a room is to use a purpose-designed essential oil vaporiser or 'burner'. They come in various shapes and sizes and in many price ranges, so you should be able to find one that is both attractive and affordable. Most are made of earthenware (sometimes glass, porcelain or marble), with decorative openings cut out of the sides to afford a free flow of air for the night-light candle which is placed inside. A small dish fits over the night light and is filled with water, then a few drops of essential oil are floated on the surface. This is gently heated by the flame. As the aromatic oil evaporates, the room becomes permeated with fragrance.

Electric vaporisers (usually called diffusers) are also available. These gadgets are particularly good for the workplace (they do not pose a fire risk) and are certainly much safer than a candle-heated vaporiser when used in the bedroom. Should you wish to vaporise oils in the bathroom, however, then obviously the nightlight vaporiser is the first and only choice. Alternatively, you may prefer to sprinkle up to six drops of essential oil into the bath water (for advice on choosing the correct bath oil(s) for your physical and emotional needs, see page 84).

The usual quantity of essential oil for most vaporisers is between four and eight drops added to the water-filled dish. The exact number of drops will depend upon the odour intensity of the individual oils used (let your nose be your guide).

PSYCHOTHERAPEUTIC AROMAS CHART

The following essences and absolutes (organic aromatics captured by means of volatile solvents rather than by steam distillation) have been categorised according to the most likely effects they may exert on the central nervous system. A few of those oils categorised as 'aphrodisiac' may have a subthreshold pheromonal influence (that is to say, they contain minute amounts of substances chemically akin to human sexual secretions). Always remember to choose according to your aroma preference. If the aroma is disliked or conjures up unpleasant memories or feelings, the conscious mind can easily override the effect of the aroma upon the mind/body.

Stimulating	Balancing (relaxing or stimulating according to state of individual)	Relaxing	Anti-depressant	Aphrodisiac	Anaphrodisiac (quells sexual desire)
angelica	basil	cedarwood	basil	angelica	camphor
black pepper	bergamot	chamomile	bergamot	cardamom	marjoram
cardamom	frankincense	clary sage	carnation	carnation	
carnation	geranium	cypress	absolute	absolute	
absolute	lavender	galbanum	chamomile	cedarwood	
cinnamon	lemongrass	hops	clary sage	cinnamon	
cloves	neroli	juniper berry	frankincense	clary sage	
elemi	rose absolute	mandarin	geranium	cloves	
eucalyptus	rose otto	marjoram	grapefruit	coriander	
fennel		mimosa absolute	jasmine absolute	galbanum	
ginger		myrrh	lavender	ginger	
grapefruit		petitgrain	lemon	jasmine absolute	
jasmine absolute		sandalwood	lime	neroli	
lime		valerian	mandarin	nutmeg	
nutmeg		vetiver	neroli	patchouli	
orange		violet leaf	orange	rose absolute	
palmarosa		absolute	palmarosa	rose otto	
patchouli		ylang ylang	patchouli	rosemary	
peppermint			petitgrain	sandalwood	
pine			rose absolute	vetiver	
rosemary			rose otto	ylang ylang	
			sandalwood		
			ylang ylang		

Some Fragrant Possibilities

We shall return to the use of essential oils for therapeutic and aesthetic purposes in subsequent chapters. In the mean time, here are a few of my own favourite room scents just to inspire you.

Sea of Tranquillity
3 drops clary sage
3 drops petitgrain
2 drops vetiver

Joie de Vivre
(*to uplift the spirit*)
3 drops mandarin
2 drops bergamot
1 drop geranium
2 drops ylang ylang

Jewel in the Lotus
(*a meditation aid*)
3 drops frankincense
3 drops cedarwood
1 drop elemi

Mensa
(*for study purposes*)
2 drops coriander
2 drops grapefruit
2 drops black pepper

Me-Oh-My Delilah!
(*an erogenic blend*)
1 drop jasmine absolute
3 drops rose absolute
3 drops sandalwood

COLOUR THERAPY

Colour therapists are convinced that certain colours can engender a state of harmony to body, mind and soul. Using a variety of techniques, from colour breathing exercises (whereby the recipient is asked to visualise a specific colour as they breathe in and out), to sophisticated light treatments (chromotherapy), they aim to reduce stress levels, and even to treat illness. In fact, there is some impressive scientific evidence to validate such claims. For example, the standard treatment for neonatal jaundice used to be a blood transfusion, but today babies are simply exposed to blue light for a period of time – a non-invasive, risk-free treatment, and it works.

Since you are unlikely to have chromotherapy equipment at home, coloured silk is an excellent alternative. It is believed to be the finest material for conveying colour vibrations to the human organism. Weather permitting, therapists recommend draping your naked body with a length of silk (in the appropriate hue) and lying in sunlight for about 20 minutes 3 times a week! To ascertain the correct shade for your needs, refer to the Healing Colour Guide given below.

If your surroundings are dull and lifeless, make every effort to improve the situation. Put fresh flowers or potted plants around the house. If possible, decorate at least one room in your home with positive and joyful colours such as shades of yellow and gold, peach, clear greens and pinks. However, do take into account the function of the room. For example, while vivacious colours like bright red, orange and yellow (in moderation) would go down well in the dining room, they would be perceived as raucus in the bedroom and likely to disrupt sleep. (Incidentally, you may find it helpful to obtain one of the many excellent books on the art of using colour in decorating.)

Similarly, try to wear uplifting colours instead of murky greys and a lot of black. Without doubt, sombre hues can aggravate depression in susceptible individuals. Indeed, it is a great pity that most school uniforms are based around black, navy and grey, colours which are hardly conducive to the exuberance (and emotional turbulence) of youth.

Healing Colour Guide

Should you feel the need for any of these colours, introduce them by wearing an article of clothing in the appropriate shade, or by employing the coloured silk method described above. If you seem to need a particular colour (or colours) more often, then most definitely incorporate the shade in your home decorating schemes.

RED

Warm and powerful, the ray of strength and vitality. Increases body temperature, libido, heartbeat and circulation. Contra-indicated for fiery personalities and those with high blood pressure or inflamed conditions. *Magenta* (a brilliant mauvish-crimson) is a highly refined variant which is better tolerated by those who find other reds garish. It boosts vitality and is an adrenal tonic (helpful for nervous exhaustion). Then there is the *pink* ray, the softest variant of red suitable for just about everyone, but especially fragile types in need of a gentle revitaliser.

▶

ORANGE

Warm and revitalising, imparting a sense of joyous rapture. Energises the thyroid gland, activates the respiratory system. Can often be used when red cannot – though like red, is contra-indicated where there is inflammation. Variants of the orange theme include *peach* (less exuberant, comforting and softening to the emotions) and *gold* (good for healing in general).

YELLOW

Warm, the ray of the intellect. A good colour for energising the muscular system and the lymphatic system, also good for a sluggish colon and for stimulating the mind. However, this colour may be too stimulating for those who suffer from nervous tension and insomnia. A variant of yellow is *cream*, which is generally regarded as a balancing colour with no contra-indications.

GREEN

Cool, the ray of harmony. Helps to allay anxiety and brings about peace and well-being. It is also a tonic, but it strengthens without stimulating. Soothes stomach and liver inflammations and calms the nerves. However, this colour is contra-indicated where there is anaemia. *Turquoise* is a variant of green and has a calming and soothing effect. It is helpful during periods of prolonged stress and where there is impaired resistance to every passing infection. A general tonic to the skin.

BLUE

Cool, the ray of inspiration and a relaxant. Relieves inflammation (particularly of the skin), helpful where there is jaundice, lowers blood pressure, cools fevers, aids restful sleep and engenders tranquillity. *Dark blue* is a variant and is said to speed the healing of broken bones and fractures. However, any shade of blue is contra-indicated where there is fatigue or depression.

INDIGO

Cool, the ray of intuition and a relaxant. Helps to reduce bleeding and excessive menstrual flow. Helpful for pain, inflammation and swelling; also tones muscles, nerves and skin. *Purple* is a variant of indigo, depressing the sex drive in order to enhance spiritual pursuits such as prayer and meditation. An inspirational colour. However, like blue, both indigo and purple are contra-indicated where there is depression.

VIOLET

Cool, the ray of spirituality and a relaxant. Stimulates the pineal gland (the 'third eye'), while sedating the central nervous system. Helpful for stress and anxiety, insomnia, skin complaints and for relieving pain. However, it is contra-indicated when energy is required or where there is deep depression. *Lavender* is a paler variant of violet and can be used to soothe stress and alleviate insomnia.

ART THERAPY

Having considered the healing power of colour in our everyday lives, it would seem appropriate at this juncture to explore the basics of therapeutic artwork. The main purpose of this mode of therapy is to provide a way in which to express our emotions other than verbally. It also enables us to access the unconscious aspect of self, especially if the artwork is expressed in some abstract form. Although there are many methods of art therapy, one of the most satisfying forms comes in the shape of the mandala.

The Way of the Mandala

It was the Swiss psychiatrist Carl Gustav Jung who proposed the reality of the psychic life, that the 'active imagination' was a path towards self-knowledge. He suggested that all human consciousness is linked together, that the consciousness of each person is like a small pond which trickles into the ocean of a shared 'collective unconscious'. The contents of this collective unconscious contain the archetypes. These are cross-cultural imprints, images and ideas that are intrinsic to the human psyche – patterns, motifs and themes which appear in myth, fairy tales and in world religions. The mandala (the sanskrit term for circle) is one such symbol.

Since ancient times, the circular motif appears as a satisfying and meaningful form of expression. Why should this be so? The circle reflects our natural history, our innate connection with the forces of nature. It represents the circular path of the earth and moon around the sun, the alternation of day and night, the rhythm of the seasons – even the subliminal memory of being encircled and firmly held in our mother's womb.

Jung was convinced of the transformative power of the mandala. As well as encouraging his patients to reveal themselves through circular artwork, he found the method extremely helpful during a difficult time in his own life. The mandala, he believed, could be used as tool for self-discovery and healing, especially during periods of transition or crisis. Mandala work enables us to focus inwards, to find some kind of direction and stability within a seemingly chaotic outer world. Moreover, the act of drawing a circle itself is symbolic of creating a sacred or protective space in which to express our innermost feelings.

Since there is no right or wrong way to create a mandala, there is no need to feel inadequate about any perceived lack of artistic skill. Each mandala (no matter how simply expressed) is a reflection of the energies moving within you. In other words, it is a representation of your emotional state at the time of its creation.

Preparation for Mandala Work

You will need some white artwork paper and colouring materials such as oil pastels, felt-tipped pens (in a wide range of colours) or paints. You may also find it helpful to have a compass for drawing a circle, or perhaps a small paper plate which can be used as a guide for the same purpose. It is also important to ensure that there is adequate light and a flat surface on which to work.

To create a conducive atmosphere, ensure that the room in which you work is comfortably warm and free of clutter and that you will not be disturbed for at least an hour. You may also wish to put on a tape or CD of gentle music and/or vaporise an appropriate essential oil (or blend). As a suggestion, you might like to try cedarwood, cypress, frankincense, juniper berry, pine or sandalwood, any of which can be enhanced by mixing with a tiny amount of lavender, clary sage or petitgrain – and perhaps a tinge of bergamot.

Now try the exercise opposite.

Interpreting Mandalas

There is no need to concern yourself with the standard psychological meanings associated with the individual symbols, colours and forms that appear in your mandalas (though the Healing Colour Guide given earlier may lead to partial insight into the meaning of your artwork). More important is the feeling evoked by the mandala as a whole – be it aggressive, gloomy, garish, morbid, joyful, tangled, serene or whatever. Quite often, the simple act of setting the imagination free is enough to trigger the process of self-healing – especially if there is no other creative outlet in your life. By creating a number of mandalas over a long period it is interesting to watch how they change and evolve.

CREATING A MANDALA

Here are the six steps in creating a mandala (adapted from the work of American art therapist, Susanne F. Fincher).

1 Before you begin, close your eyes for a few moments and breathe out with a sigh, allowing all tension and thoughts of the day to melt away.

2 Next begin to focus inwards, becoming aware of any feelings, forms, colours and shapes that may come to the fore. If nothing emerges, simply go on to the next step.

3 Open your eyes and look at the colours before you. Choose a colour with which to begin drawing your mandala – any colour that leaps into your vision. Next, make a circle using a compass or a paper plate as a guide. Or, if you prefer, draw the circle freehand.

4 Continue by filling in the circle with colour and form, perhaps starting in the centre or maybe around the inner edge of the circle. You may find yourself creating a concentric pattern in just a few colours, or some other organised design. On the other hand, your mandala may reveal many weird and wonderful shapes in a variety of hues. Continue working until you feel your mandala is complete.

5 When you feel ready, imagine yourself very small and pretend that you are walking into the image as if it were a room or a landscape. Once inside, ask yourself how it feels to be there. Where are you most/least comfortable, and what do your symbols look like from this perspective?

6 Having experienced your feelings and thoughts within the mandala, you might like to give it a name. Write the name at the bottom of the drawing, along with the date (helpful for future reference).

In the words of Susanne Fincher: 'The way of the mandala is an active meditation for the purposes of personal growth and spiritual enrichment . . . its symbolic language enables us to go deeper into the meaning of who we really are'. (If you would like to learn more about this fascinating path to self-knowledge, refer to the Suggested Reading list).

3

Promoting Health and Vitality

*I*N THIS chapter we shall explore the ways in which we may strengthen our defences against stress, replenish our energies and promote long-term health and vitality. Although ostensibly viewed from the physical perspective – emphasising such things as healthy eating, adequate exercise, dry skin brushing and massage – in reality it is impossible to separate the mind from the body. As we have already seen, body and mind are interrelated; whatever affects one aspect of our being – the body, mind or spirit – affects the whole.

FOOD

What exactly is a 'well-balanced diet'? This is a difficult question to answer, for none of the experts seem able to agree. One minute we are told to avoid all animal fat because it is bad for the heart and to opt for polyunsaturated cooking oils and soft margarines such as sunflower or soya. The next moment we are told that, far from being healthy alternatives, many highly refined vegetable oils, low-fat spreads and other margarines actually contribute to the build-up of 'bad' cholesterol in the body (there is also 'good' cholesterol) and hence to the development of heart disease.

So, nutritionists are now urging that we go back to eating a little butter in preference to margarine, and to using moderate quantities of *unrefined* vegetable oils such as extra virgin olive, sunflower seed and sesame. Unlike processed fats and highly refined cooking oils, unrefined or cold-pressed oils have been a dietary staple for thousands of years; therefore, they are highly compatible with the human digestive system.

Sugar

Sugar is another bone of contention. In recent years we have been told to avoid all types, whether it be in the form of honey, molasses, unrefined muscovado or refined, white sugar. This has led to the widescale use of artificial sweeteners such as aspartame, marketed under the brand names NutraSweet and Equal. Its predecessors, such as cyclamate and saccharin, have been implicated as known or possible carcinogens – cancer-causing substances – but aspartame has so far received a clean bill of health. However, there are a few researchers who are concerned about the possible risks of aspartame. A study carried out at the D.C. Children's Hospital in the USA, for example, suggests that it may trigger hyperactive or manic behaviour in susceptible youngsters.

Amazingly, and contrary to the conclusions of earlier research, the latest findings suggest that a small amount of unrefined muscovado sugar is actually good for us. Moreover, far from being the number one enemy of teeth and gums, dark muscovado sugar (not the refined artificially coloured type which masquerades as the real thing) is said to *prevent* tooth decay – a view which had been advocated by health food pioneers in the 1950s.

Supplements and Different Diets

And while a great many nutritionists advocate taking vitamin and mineral supplements, others believe that we can obtain all the nutrients we need from the food we eat – assuming that we follow the latest dietary recommendations. Certainly, nutritional supplements should never be regarded as an alternative to a healthy diet. A vitamin C tablet, for example, is not as welcome to the digestive system, nor as pleasing to the psyche, as a bowl of fruit salad.

Nevertheless, there may be a place for supplements to help boost the immune system during periods of ill health or prolonged stress, and perhaps for a month or two afterwards to aid recovery. At such times we utilise certain nutrients at a higher than usual level. Most nutritionists would agree that a good multi-vitamin and mineral formula containing the entire B-complex range of nutrients is always a good insurance policy.

Returning to the question of what constitutes a healthy diet, my own response to the mass of contradictions surrounding the subject is to suggest there is no one ideal diet suitable for everyone. We are each very different, with varying physiological needs and personal philosophies. Whatever we may believe about diet, the only clear-cut rule, as far as I see it, is that our food should be as free as possible from the toxic residues of modern farming methods – no easy task nowadays.

However, organically produced foods are a rarity. Even when they are available they can be expensive, prohibitively so for some people. The best thing we can do, until organically grown produce becomes the norm, is to eat foods as near as possible to their natural state – not out of tins and packets whose contents may be doused in white sugar, excessive salt, monosodium glutamate and other potentially harmful additives.

The steps on pages 67–8 outline a wholefood diet as recommended by many aware nutritionists. It does not take into account food allergies – some people are allergic to wheat dairy products or nuts, for example – or if you wish to avoid animal foods altogether (veganism) or whether you prefer not to eat meat and fish (vegetarianism). It should, however, serve as a useful guide that can be adapted to suit individual needs. Aim to alter your diet gradually over a period of six months. Drastic overnight changes will almost certainly lead to digestive upsets.

Food and Mood

Until recently, the only known method of helping to balance mood was through a variety of drugs with undesirable side-effects. Only when scientists started to examine what the brain and nervous system were actually made of did the importance of nutrition become apparant in emotional stability. The brain is made entirely out of food molecules such as complex essential fatty acids, vitamins, minerals, proteins and other nutrients.

A growing number of nutritional therapists such as Patrick Holford, the director of the Institute for Optimum Nutrition in the UK, are convinced that a nutritional approach can alleviate a wide range of emotional and mental imbalances, including hyperactivity, learning difficulties, delinquent behaviour, depression,

GUIDE TO HEALTHY EATING

• Buy organically grown food if you can, but don't fret if you can't. Worrying too much about your diet will only lead to stress, which can be more harmful than a few additives.

• Eat wholemeal bread and other complex carbohydrates such as dried beans, lentils, nuts, seeds (e.g sunflower, pumpkin, sesame), wholemeal pasta, oats, brown rice and other wholegrain cereals. If dried beans, lentils, nuts and seeds cause excessive flatulence, try sprouting them in a purpose-designed salad sprouter (available from health shops) to break down the chemicals responsible for causing intestinal gas. Sprouted beans can be eaten raw in salads or added to soups, stews and casseroles. Sprouted seeds are also packed with vitamins and minerals.

• Eat plenty of fruit and vegetables – preferably unskinned, well scrubbed and raw in salads or lightly cooked. Frozen fruits and vegetables are fine as an occasional stand-by, especially during the winter months when fresh produce may be in short supply, but they should not form the basis of your daily diet.

• Cut down on all fats, particularly those from animal sources, especially lard, suet, double cream, butter and full-fat cheese. As much as possible, eschew any product that has been hydrogenated or highly processed. Use moderate amounts of cold-pressed vegetable oils such as extra virgin olive, sesame and sunflower seed (about one tablespoonful each day) in salad dressings. If you intend to cook with oil, the most stable is olive (both the 'extra virgin' and 'virgin' grades). It does not break down during storage or cooking to create substances that harm essential fatty acids in the body. But keep in the fridge and use up before the recommended date.

• Cut down on milk, whether full-fat or skimmed. The most digestible is probably organically produced goats' milk, which those normally allergic to dairy products (eczema sufferers, for example) can often tolerate. Live, full-fat plain yoghurt (preferably organic) is good for most people, whether it comes from the cow, goat or sheep.

• Sweeten your foods sparingly with honey (preferably raw or unheated honey) or a little unrefined muscovado sugar, or more lavishly with dried fruits such as dates, figs, sultanas and raisins.

▶

● Cut down on salt (even sea salt should be used sparingly), and use more herbs and spices to flavour your food. A high-salt diet can be a contributing factor in the development of high blood pressure and oedema (fluid retention). Salt occurs naturally in most foods, so there is no such thing as a completely salt-free diet, but by not adding salt to your food you can achieve a low-salt diet.

● Buy free-range eggs if possible.

● Eat red meat only occasionally, if at all. Instead, eat free-range poultry and fish, particularly oily fish such as mackerel.

● Try to avoid processed foods in cans and packets as far as possible because these are usually laden with chemical additives. They will do no harm as an occasional stand-by but should not form the basis of your daily diet.

● A little red or white wine (preferably organic) is good for the digestive system and can help normalise blood cholesterol levels. Between one and three glasses a day is the recommended quantity.

● Drink plenty of water (bottled or filtered), herb teas and diluted fruit juices. If you cannot give up ordinary tea or coffee altogether (they can contribute to stress-related symptoms), try to limit your intake to no more than two cups of coffee a day, or three cups of tea. Decaffeinated versions may be laden with chemicals employed in the process – unless, that is, the label specifically states that the caffeine has been removed by water-extraction.

● It is fine to err once in a while, to indulge in the occasional chocolate bar, Danish pastry or fry up. And there is no need to feel guilty about it either. It is only when such indulgences become a daily habit at the expense of more nutritious foods that they constitute a health hazard.

● Throw away the scales and forget about counting calories, especially if you are stuck in a diet/binge cycle. Enlightened nutritionists now realise that people have very different metabolisms – while there are those who can eat vast quantities and remain slim, others certainly cannot. If you are very overweight for no apparent reason, you may be suffering from hidden food allergies, in which case, do seek the advice of a holistic nutritionist (see Useful Addresses).

● Eat slowly in convivial surroundings and, above all, enjoy your food!

anxiety, insomnia, anorexia, memory loss, even schizophrenia. Rather than giving drugs which block the action of neuro-transmitters (brain hormones), says Holford, it is possible to give the body the raw materials it needs for the brain to rebalance its own chemistry.

Even as far back as the 1960s, Canadian researchers Drs Hoffer and Osmond were able to demonstrate that certain forms of schizophrenia could be effectively treated through specific diets and nutritional supplements. Moreover, mental health research over the last few decades has proven that food allergies or intolerance can also result in mental and emotional symptoms.

Serious mental imbalance aside (for its treatment requires expert intervention), everyone can benefit from the mood-enhancing (and therefore stress-reducing) effects of food. The first step in balancing brain chemistry, and thus the way we perceive the world, is to alkalise the blood and keep blood sugar levels up. The first can be achieved through a diet largely comprising fresh fruits, salad greens, herbs and other vegetables. The latter depends upon timing of meals. Some people need to eat little and often – maybe five meals a day – to stabilise blood sugar levels and to keep their emotions on an even keel. These snacks should consist of high-energy foods like dried fruits, nuts, seeds and wholemeal bread.

Studies have also shown that eating a high carbohydrate, low protein meal favours the uptake of tryptophan in the brain. Tryptophan is a precursor to the neuro-transmitter serotonin, which is important for relaxation and for inducing sleep. Good sources include bananas and wholemeal bread.

A high protein meal, say, a large steak and green salad, tends to lower serotonin production in the brain. It also increases tyrosine, a precursor nutrient which triggers the production of cate-cholamine brain hormones. These chemicals are associated with energetic 'stressed' states and are inclined to make us feel mentally and physically active. They are also associated with feelings of power, control and domination. Moreover, foods such as soya products and eggs make us feel more alert because they contain lecithin, the precurser for acetylcholine, a stimulating neuro-transmitter.

It is important to point out that all the tests have been carried out on people who eat the foods on an empty stomach. So a meal which contains eggs, but also such foods as potatoes, bread and sugar, is unlikely to have the same stimulating effect. Researchers have also discovered that women are much more susceptible to the sleep-inducing effects of a high carbohydrate meal, while men tend to experience only a pleasant calmness following the same type of meal. Men are also more likely to become highly alert after eating a protein-rich meal.

The differences in sex hormones and body composition is the probable explanation for specifically 'male' and 'female' mood responses to food chemicals. Women have larger amounts of oestrogen and a higher percentage of body fat, whereas men have larger quantities of testosterone, smaller fat cells and greater muscle mass. This means women are especially responsive to the soporific effects of carbohydrate foods, which help maintain the body's fat reserves, and men are more responsive to the mood-elevating effect of protein foods, which are essential for building, repairing and synthesising muscle.

Nutrients for a Positive Outlook

All vitamins and minerals play a part in optimum brain function, but some are especially influential in promoting a positive outlook:

Vitamin B-complex

By improving the circulation, this group of nutrients ensures that the brain is well supplied with oxygen-rich blood which, in turn, enhances clarity of thought and better enables us to cope in the face of adversity. Good sources of B vitamins include wholegrain products, egg yolks, fish, nuts, dried beans, bean curd (tofu), cheese, yoghurt and brewer's yeast.

Vitamin C

This is important in the synthesis of anti-stress hormones. It is found in all fresh fruits and vegetables, especially blackcurrants, citrus fruits, peppers and broccoli.

Magnesium

A deficiency of magnesium causes irritability, nervousness and depression. Good sources of this mineral are found in dairy foods, meat and seafood.

▶

Manganese

This nutrient works in conjunction with the B-complex vitamins to ensure a healthy nervous system. It is found in foods such as avocados, nuts, seeds, seaweed, wholegrain products, egg yolks, salad greens and pineapples.

Zinc

As well as being important to the functions of taste and smell, this nutrient is vital to the proper functioning of the immune system. A deficiency can lead to a broad spectrum of problems ranging from poor appetite, abnormalities of taste and smell, through to under-functioning sex glands and mental lethargy. Good dietary sources of zinc include pumpkin seeds, nuts, wholegrains, brewer's yeast, egg yolks, seafoods, meat and poultry.

Then there are those foods which contain the mood elevating chemical phenylethlamine (PEA) – chocolate, cheese and salami, for example. Other food substances such as fennel, peppermint, rosemary and horseradish contain stimulating chemicals.

Of course, our moods are not entirely governed by what we ate for lunch. Moods are always both chemical and psychological, moving in response to the dictates of our own guiding impulse. Indeed, even when a person is suffering from a biochemically based depression, they must still learn psychological skills in order to cope with life, moods and feelings.

Herbs for Stress-Related Ailments

The herbs shown on the chart below are especially helpful for stress-related ailments. However, in a body congested with the debris of a junk food diet, cigarette smoke and the excesses of a frenetic lifestyle, they are unlikely to make much impact. Compared with conventional medicines, most herbal remedies work very gently. Therefore, in order to derive maximum benefit from them, they need to be incorporated as part of an holistic healing programme.

If you have a garden, you may wish to grow your own medicinal and culinary herbs. As well as being attractive, most aromatic herbs are easy to grow and they demand little space. Some will also thrive in pots and other containers. Alternatively, dried herbs can be obtained from most health shops or from herbal suppliers. But what about herbal tablets and capsules?

My own feeling is that tasting and smelling the medicine is an essential part of the treatment, especially when dealing with digestive upsets. For example, certain constituents collectively known as bitters (found in peppermint and sage) promote the flow of saliva and gastric juices in a complex way via the taste buds and a reflex action in the brain. This action is by-passed when the remedy is taken in tablet or capsule form.

With the exception of sage, which should be avoided during pregnancy, the herbs featured are perfectly safe – that is, provided the recommended dosages are not greatly exceeded. It is advisable, however, to seek the advice of a qualified medical herbalist before administering herbal remedies to infants and young children. To make an infusion or herb tea, you will need about three tea-spoonsful of the bruised fresh herb per cup (bruise in a pestle and mortar) or one teasponful of dried. Then pour boiling water over the herbs and allow to steep for 10–15 minutes. A little honey can be added if desired. The usual dosage is a teacupful three times a day.

Herbs for Stress-Related Ailments

Herb	Therapeutic effect
Chamomile, Roman (*Chamaemelum nobile*)	A gentle sedative. Helpful for anxiety and insomnia; also headaches and digestive upsets. The cooled tea can also be used as an eye wash for soothing tired and itchy eyes.
Lavender (*Lavendula officinalis*)	Promotes natural sleep. Also helpful for headaches, depression and nervous tension. The cooled tea can also be applied as a lotion for minor stress-related skin rashes.
Lemon Balm (*Melissa officinalis*)	Helpful for anxiety, depression and nervous tension.

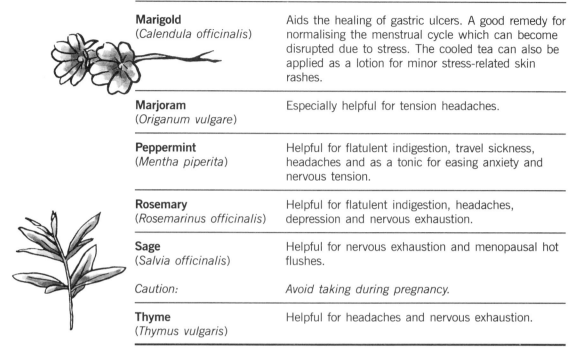

Marigold (*Calendula officinalis*)	Aids the healing of gastric ulcers. A good remedy for normalising the menstrual cycle which can become disrupted due to stress. The cooled tea can also be applied as a lotion for minor stress-related skin rashes.
Marjoram (*Origanum vulgare*)	Especially helpful for tension headaches.
Peppermint (*Mentha piperita*)	Helpful for flatulent indigestion, travel sickness, headaches and as a tonic for easing anxiety and nervous tension.
Rosemary (*Rosemarinus officinalis*)	Helpful for flatulent indigestion, headaches, depression and nervous exhaustion.
Sage (*Salvia officinalis*) *Caution:*	Helpful for nervous exhaustion and menopausal hot flushes. *Avoid taking during pregnancy.*
Thyme (*Thymus vulgaris*)	Helpful for headaches and nervous exhaustion.

The Food of Love

If your libido needs a lift, forget the powdered rhino horn, elixir of ruby or Spanish fly – the latest research into food and fragrance suggests looking no further than the local delicatessen. According to Australian explorer of the senses, Dr Max Lake, and osmologist (expert on the sense of smell) Dr George Dodd, certain foods are decidedly erotic, emanating libidinous pheromones (hormone-like odorants) which mimic our own sexual secretions. Some foods produce an attractively musky odour which emanates from the skin some hours after eating – asparagus, celeriac, cooked chestnuts, coriander leaves, sweetcorn, parsley, parsnips, truffles and wild mushrooms.

Pungent spices are all reputed aphrodisiacs due to their warming, stimulating effect. The most potent are black pepper,

cardamom, cumin, cinnamon, clove, coriander, fenugreek, green chillies, ginger, nutmeg and turmeric. And for many people, the seductive taste and aroma of vanilla, especially when combined with chocolate, promotes the contentment of post-coital bliss.

Fresh yeasty bread is analogous with and complementary to the smell of a clean body. But some foods emanate an overtly faecal note, repellent to some, erotic to others. Faecal odours are found in asafoetida, an Indian curry spice, and durian, an exotic fruit with a notorious reputation! Surprisingly, jasmine flowers (used to flavour a certain kind of Indian tea) and orange flower water (delightful in fruit salads) have this same odour nuance, albeit at sub-threshold levels. Even the seemingly innocent scent of rose-water, the authentic Turkish delight flavouring, contains an erotic 'sweaty' note. It also harbours phenylethylalcohol, which derives from the mood elevating substance PEA.

Sweet and mellow foods – bananas, chocolate, almond, cashew nuts, creamed coconut and dairy ice-cream – are reputedly aphrodisiac because they have 'mouth feel'. But how can something as cold as ice-cream be deemed erogenic? The answer is that its coldness gives an initial charge of excitement – an awakening of the senses – followed by a sensuous sweet, smooth afterglow as it warms in the mouth.

A glass of good wine tantalises the senses and triggers an immediate rush. It combines colour, bouquet, taste, subliminal pain (if sparkling), plus the effects of the alcohol itself, which can help lessen inhibitions. Wine from the red grape sauvignon scents the whole body within six hours of drinking. Any wine that has been aged in oak barrels produces an erotic musky odour nuance. The wine also absorbs vanillin from the wood, giving a seductive tinge of vanilla. And, as if that were not enough, good wine also contains an appreciable quantity of sensual grape pheromones.

Believe it or not, even the humble green pea has a place in Aphrodite's larder. Fresh green peas are endowed with isobutyl methoxy pyraxine (IMP), a mischievous odour nuance that women especially find irresistible. IMP is also found in freshly cut grass – which may explain why 'love among the haystacks' is so exciting!

The Problem with Dieting

Most people, especially women, who lose weight on a diet soon regain the weight – and often more besides. It seems that women's bodies in particular are designed to sabotage diets. For the purpose of reproduction, their bodies naturally have, and need, more body fat. So when a woman tries to survive on a low calorie diet, sooner or later she will probably resort to binge eating.

As well as compromising health and well-being, stringent dieting – especially yo-yo crash dieting – is counter-productive in another way: it slows down the rate at which the body burns calories. Even when such a person starts eating normally again, they are likely to gain weight more easily because their body has become super-efficient at storing fat.

Moreover, researchers at Littlemore Hospital, Oxford (UK), studied a group of women on a 1,000 calorie-a-day diet, and found that there were definite changes in brain chemistry which made the dieters feel frustrated and miserable. This is because stringent dieting causes a reduction in the level of serotonin. As indicated earlier, serotonin is associated with calmness and mood stability.

Should stringent dieting become a way of life, it may even lead to heart disease and angina, or develop into an eating disorder such as anorexia nervosa or bulimia (binge eating followed by purging and vomiting). While eating disorders claim females in particular, males are by no means immune. Although the underlying cause may be more complex, the greatest pressure must surely come from modern society's obsession with the Body Beautiful – an impossibly thin (or muscular) ideal which few people could possibly hope to achieve, at least not without a masochistic regime of self-denial with the inevitable accompanying stress.

With the daily bombardment of slimming propaganda from the media, largely aimed at lining the pockets of the diet-food industry, it is with great reluctance that I mention weight-reduction in this book (a stress-inducing topic for many people). Just for the record, however, those who successfully lose weight certainly do not starve themselves. Instead, they increase their activity level. The latter is partly due to calorie-burning, but there is also a psychological element – they feel they are taking charge of their lives.

MOVEMENT

Moderate but persistent activity can exert a wonderful effect upon the mind/body complex. It strengthens the heart and lungs, stimulates circulation, increases flexibility in muscles and joints, improves the quality of sleep, reduces stress and enhances a sense of well-being.

To many people, however, 'exercise' connotes strenuous movement performed with a tense and determined expression – as seen in the wrist-watching jogger or grimacing weight-trainer. This is a peculiarly Western idea of what beneficial movement is all about. The ideal is to balance the whole system, mind and body. This can be achieved by a brisk half-hour walk every day, for example, or by some other form of movement that you actively enjoy. So long as you do not overdo it, you will experience revitalisation rather than a depletion of energy.

My own approach is to favour natural outdoor activities such as hill walking, gardening and swimming – preferably in unpolluted rivers, lakes or seas. Of course, not everyone has a garden or lives within easy reach of such wild and beautiful places. For the city dweller, or for those who do not derive any special pleasure from such activities, other forms of movement like dancing (any style to suit your own taste and stamina), cycling (preferably away from main roads), keep-fit, dance aerobics, football, tennis or some other energetic sport can be taken up instead.

However, if you have a high powered job which encourages you to compete in the market place, it is certainly not advisable to take up a competitive sport. The stress of the competition will cancel out the benefits of the exercise.

If you are elderly, have a disability or are too ill to take much exercise, do not despair: regular massage (see pages 92–103) given by a friend with 'good hands' (or a professional massage therapist if you can afford it) can be almost as beneficial. Another excellent alternative is dry skin brushing (see page 83). If such measures are employed in conjunction with a healthy diet, fresh air and moderate exposure to sunlight (up to an hour a day in the summer months), you will experience renewed vitality.

Yoga

A good all-rounder for body, mind and soul is the ancient discipline of yoga. Ideally, you should join a class headed by a qualified teacher who will monitor your progress and ensure that you do not pull any muscles. You will also be shown how to breathe correctly – a vital aspect of the art. There is no need to twist your body into weird and wonderful shapes or to stand on your head in order to benefit from yoga. Indeed, many people take up the art in their later years and have neither the ambition nor the ability to become contortionists. Just learning the basics of good breathing, conscious relaxation (as described in Chapter 1) and stretching is enough to revitalise your whole being.

The following yoga sequence differs from other yoga asanas (postures) because each pose is held for just a few seconds, one following on from the other in a continuous movement, whereas yoga asanas are usually held for at least 30 seconds. Although it looks quite complicated, with practice you will soon be able to perform the sequence as a flowing movement with synchronised breathing. If you are reasonably supple, you should have little difficulty bending into each position.

However, if your muscles and joints are unused to this type of exercise, it is essential to take it slowly, only bending as far as your body will allow without causing pain. Indeed, the emphasis is not on perfect performance, but on the ability to focus inwards through breathing and movement. Whatever you achieve is right for you. Indeed, the 'no pain, no gain' approach is a myth. Repeat the entire sequence 2 or 3 times. As your stamina and flexibility increase, eventually you will enjoy performing 10 or even 12 rounds, 3 or 4 times a week.

Perform the following sequence in the morning before breakfast or, if more convenient, late afternoon before your evening meal. If practised regularly it will lubricate the joints, improve circulation, massage the internal organs and increase strength and suppleness. At the same time, you will experience increased optimism and vitality.

SUN SALUTATION (SURYA NAMASKAR)

Take off your shoes and wear comfortable, loose clothing so as not to restrict your breathing or hinder leg movement. To enhance the atmosphere, you may wish to vaporise essential oils which suggest bright flowers, fruits and sunlight. Choose one or two of your favourites from the following list. *Instructions for vaporising essential oils are to be found on page 56.*

SUGGESTED ESSENTIAL OILS

bergamot	orange
mandarin	grapefruit
coriander	geranium
rose	lemongrass
palmarosa	

1 Stand erect with your feet together and your hands in a prayer position held at the solar plexus (midriff). Look straight ahead.

2 As you slowly breathe in, raise your arms overhead; bend back to arch your spine.

3 On the exhalation, bend forward as far as you can go without strain. If possible, place your hands flat on the floor beside your feet (or as far down as your body will comfortably allow). Let your knees bend and soften if this helps. Indeed, only very flexible people should attempt to do this movement with straight legs as it may cause pain and spasm in the lower back.

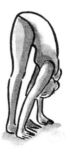

4 Inhale. Move your right leg in a backward step, your knee touching the floor. The left knee should be between the hands with the foot flat on the floor. Look straight ahead. (When repeating the exercise, remember to reverse position of legs.)

5 Holding on to the breath, and without shifting the right leg, raise the knee off the floor then move the left leg in a backward step to meet the right foot. Toes are turned in and the body is elevated into a 'press up' position, but with the arms fully stretched and the palms flat on the floor. Look straight ahead.

6 Exhale. Gently bend your knees to touch the floor and slowly slide the body down so that forehead and chest come into contact with the floor.

7 On the inhalation, straighten your legs and bend backwards, looking up at the ceiling with arms straight, elbows close to the body and palms firmly on the floor.

8 As you exhale, arch your back into a cat's stretch, head down between your arms. Do not strain, keep your head limp.

9 Inhale. Bring the right leg forward alongside the palms. The left foot and knee should touch the floor. (When repeating the exercise, reverse the position of the legs.)

10 On the exhalation, bend forward until your hands are in line with your feet (or as far down as your body will allow). Tighten your abdomen and bring your head as close as possible to your knees, allowing the knees to bend a little to ease the movement.

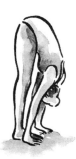

12 As you exhale, lower your arms to your sides.

11 As you inhale, raise your arms overhead; bend back to arch your spine.

Once you have completed a few rounds of the sequence, with a 30-second rest between each cycle, lie down on a firm surface (for example, the floor covered with a thick blanket or a yoga mat) and allow yourself to let go completely. Lie there for at least five minutes, allowing your breathing and pulse rate to return to normal. When you feel ready, have a good stretch from fingertips to toes; roll over to one side and slowly get up.

NATURAL LIGHT

Light is as essential to life as food and water. It is absorbed by our bodies and used in a whole range of metabolic processes. Artificial light is vastly inferior, lacking the full colour spectrum of the ultra violet rays of daylight, and has been blamed for a number of ailments suffered by indoor workers. The most common problems associated with full-spectrum light deprivation are perpetual tiredness, headaches, irritability, lack of concentration and a cyclic mental state known as seasonal affective disorder (SAD).

Psychiatrists first became aware that some people suffer severe winter depression as a result of light deprivation half a century ago, but the disorder has only recently been treated seriously. As well as the symptoms mentioned above, sufferers of SAD may experience loss of libido and self-esteem, overeating and what can best be described as 'sleepaholism'. The gloom begins to descend in the autumn, reaching an all-time low mid-winter, only to magically lift again with the first rays of spring sunshine.

SAD sufferers are hypersensitive to reduced sunlight. When light enters our eyes it strikes the pineal gland in the brain, which secretes melatonin – the substance which affects sleep, mood and the reproductive cycle. Usually levels of melatonin rise at night and subside at dawn. In SAD, melatonin production happens later at night than usual, resulting in a 'sleep hangover' and all-day blues.

If you suffer from a mild form of the winter blues (as is most common), and are forced to spend a great deal of time indoors, it might be worth investing in some full-spectrum lighting – that which mimics natural daylight for it contains all the colours of the rainbow. Severe cases respond best to very bright full-spectrum light emitted from a purpose-designed unit or 'light-box'. The sufferer basks in front of the light first thing in the morning, which serves to kick-start the body for the rest of the day. Studies have shown that full-spectrum light treatment (phototherapy) has an impressive 85 per cent success rate. Full-spectrum light bulbs and light-boxes can be obtained by mail order (see Useful Addresses).

Even on a cloudy day, there is always more light outside than indoors. Whether or not you are suffering from SAD, a daily half-hour walk in the countryside or the local park will contribute to a sense of well-being.

What about sunbathing? Even though ultra violet light has had a bad press in recent years, due to the risks of cateracts and skin cancer, a certain amount is good for us. As well as elevating mood, it causes a photo-chemical response in the skin which triggers the formation of vitamin D. This nutrient is essential for the absorption of calcium and other minerals which contribute to the development of strong bones and teeth.

It may come as a surprise to learn that proponents of nature cure still advocate sunbathing without the use of a sunscreen – but for limited periods. This can be anything from 5 to 20 minutes according to individual sensitivity. Most important: the sun bath should always be taken before noon or after four o'clock in the afternoon when the sun's rays are longer and less likely to burn. Of course, if you intend to stay in the sun for an hour or longer (though this is not recommended) it is essential to apply a high factor sunscreen – even if you are of Asian or African descent.

People with fair or sensitive skin may not be able to sunbathe at all. Yet they can still benefit from the energising effects of ultra violet light while sitting in the shade covered in thin cotton garments.

Air Bathing

We often forget that the skin is an organ of respiration (and also excretion), hence it is sometimes called the 'third lung'. This means that it is important to allow the skin to breathe by wearing natural fibres, at least directly against the skin (synthetics trap perspiration and hinder the free flow of air) and to avoid excessive use of chemical deodorants, anti-perspirants and skin-clogging lotions and potions.

TAKING AN AIR BATH

A popular European nature cure method for replenishing energy and imparting a sense of well-being is the 'air bath'. Simply spend between 5 and 20 minutes a day (depending on the temperature) completely unclothed, preferably outside. If this is not possible, take your air bath in a room in which the windows are wide open.

Dry Skin Brushing

Dry skin brushing is another well-proven nature cure method and one which is gaining in popularity. Not only does it help the condition of the skin itself by whisking away the build-up of dead skin cells on the surface, it stimulates lymphatic drainage and the elimination of as much as one-third of body wastes. Complaints such as arthritis, cellulite (characterised by dimpled 'orange peel' skin which is cold to the touch), high blood pressure and even depression have been linked to poor lymphatic drainage. Although dry skin brushing cannot totally replace adequate exercise, it is in fact similar in body stimulation terms to a good massage or 20 minutes' jogging!

You will need a purpose-designed vegetable bristle brush with a long, but detachable handle so that you can reach your back. These are available from many good health shops or from some chemists. If you cannot obtain a body brush, a hemp glove is a good alternative. The body needs to be brushed once a day for a few minutes before your morning bath or shower. It is a good idea to take a week's break every month as skin brushing, like many other natural detoxification techniques, is more effective if the body does not become too accustomed to it.

HOW TO DRY BRUSH YOUR SKIN

To brush your skin, make sweeping movements over each part of the body, excepting the face and neck. The skin in these places is too sensitive for the body brush treatment. Be gentle; brush too vigorously, especially if you are unused to body brushing, and you will scratch your skin. Begin with your feet, including the soles, then move up your legs, front and back, with long sweeping strokes. Brush over the buttocks and up to the mid-back. That is, always work towards the heart and bring toxins towards the colon. Then brush your hands front and back, up the arms, across the shoulders, down the chest (avoiding the nipples if you are a woman) and then brush downwards over the upper back. Finally brush the abdomen (avoiding the genitals) using a clockwise circular motion following the shape of the colon.

Skin brushing need take no longer than five minutes each time and can be done while you run the bath.

CAUTION: Do not brush where there is eczema, psoriasis or areas of broken or infected skin. You can brush where the skin is healthy, but avoid brushing over varicose veins.

Aromatic Baths

We all know that a long soak in the bath at the end of a hectic day is sheer bliss, but there are many other benefits to be gained from bathing. If you are fortunate enough to live in a house where the water comes directly from an underground spring (as is the case in many rural areas) then it will be especially health-giving. While it may lack the miraculous powers attributed to the waters of Lourdes, certainly it will be much kinder to the skin than chlorinated tap water. Nevertheless, mains water can be made more vibrant with the addition of essential oils.

PREPARING AN AROMATIC BATH

Having established which oil (or blend) would best suit your needs (see the Aromatic Profiles below), sprinkle four to eight drops on to the water's surface after the bath has been drawn. Agitate the water to disperse the oil. If you add the essential oil while the water is running, much of the aromatic vapour will have evaporated before you enter the bath. If you have dry skin, you may wish to mix the essential oil with a few teaspoonsful of a vegetable base oil such as sweet almond, sunflower seed or hazelnut, but only if you do not mind cleaning an oily bath afterwards. Neat essences never leave a greasy tide mark due to their tiny molecular structure.

Alternate Hot and Cold Shower

While baths are wonderful for winding down, showers are best if you need a wake-up treatment. If you are hardy, you will enjoy the special effects of the alternate hot and cold shower – an excellent treatment for stimulating the circulation and toning the muscles. Begin with lukewarm water, gradually increasing the heat for a couple of minutes, then change quickly to cold for 15 seconds. Repeat two or three times.

AROMATIC PROFILES

The oils profiled below are 12 of the most popular used in aromatherapy. They are also the essences which tend to feature most in stress-reducing treatments. Choose according to your condition, but always take into account your aroma preference (you may also wish to refer to the Psychotherapeutic Aromatherapy chart on page 57). A wide selection of essential oils can be found in most health shops or they can be obtained by mail order from specialist suppliers (see Useful Addresses).

Instructions for using essential oils in the bath are to be found above. For advice on preparing essential oils for massage, see page 91. If you would prefer to vaporise essential oils as mood-enhancing room scents, see page 56.

	Source and description	Aromatherapy uses	Blending suggestions	Caution
Bergamot (*Citrus bergamia*)	Extracted by means of cold expression from the skin of the tiny orange-like fruit. The aroma is citrus with a hint of spice. Its odour effect is uplifting and refreshing.	Cold and flu symptoms, anxiety, depression, pre-menstrual distress.	To enhance its uplifting, anti-depressant properties blend with lavender and geranium. To reinforce its ability to combat cold and flu symptoms, blend with eucalyptus or tea tree oil.	Avoid using this oil on the skin shortly before exposure to natural or simulated sunlight as it may cause pigmentation. Alternatively, try to obtain bergamot FCF (furocoumarin-free), a rectified version free of photo-toxic substances.
Chamomile, Roman (*Chamaemelum nobile*)	Distilled from the flower heads of the low-growing herb with white daisy-like flowers. The aroma is sweet and dry with an apple-like tinge. The odour effect is warming and calming.	Skin care (most skin types), inflamed skin conditions, muscular aches and pains, pre-menstrual syndrome, headache, insomnia, nervous tension.	To enhance its sedative effect, blend with a little clary sage and neroli. To support its muscle relaxant and anti-inflammatory properties mix with a little geranium.	Avoid during the first trimester of pregnancy.

	Source and descripton	Aromatherapy uses	Blending suggestions	Caution
Clary Sage (*Salvia sclarea*)	Distilled from the white, violet or pink flowers of the shrubby herb. The aroma is sweetly herbaceous and nutty with a floral tinge. Its odour effect is uplifting and relaxing; a reputed aphrodisiac.	High blood pressure, respiratory ailments, irregular menstruation, pre-menstrual syndrome, depression, migraine, insomnia, nervous tension and stress-related disorders.	To enhance its ability to uplift the spirits, blend with a little rose otto and lavender. To reinforce its ability to help respiratory ailments like bronchitis and catarrh, blend with frankincense and bergamot.	Avoid during pregnancy.
Frankincense (*Boswellia carterii*)	Distilled from the hardened exudations (oleo gum resin) of a small tree native to the Middle East. The aroma is warm and balsamic with a hint of lemon and camphor. The odour effect is warming, head-clearing and calming.	Skin care (particularly mature skin), respiratory ailments, painful menstruation, nervous tension and stress-related disorders.	To increase its ability to reduce nervous tension, blend with sandalwood and a tiny amount of rose otto. To support its ability to ease painful menstruation, mix with rosemary and juniper berry.	Avoid during the first trimester of pregnancy.
Geranium (*Pelargonium graveolens*)	Distillation of the leaves and flowers of the aromatic shrub commonly known as 'rose geranium'. The aroma is piercingly sweet and rosy with an unexpected hint of mint. The odour effect is refreshing and uplifting.	Skin care (most skin types), poor circulation, menopausal symptoms, pre-menstrual syndrome, nervous tension and stress-related disorders.	To enhance its uplifting, anti-depressant properties, blend with petitgrain and lavender. To reinforce its ability to improve poor circulation, mix with rosemary.	

	Source and descripton	Aromatherapy uses	Blending suggestions	Caution
Juniper Berry (*Juniperus communis*)	Distillation of the dried berries of the small evergreen conifer tree. The aroma is fresh and woody with a peppery overtone. Its odour effect is uplifting to the spirits, warming and calming.	Skin and hair care (oily), arthritic and rheumatic aches and pains, painful menstruation, nervous tension and other stress-related disorders.	To support its ability to soothe nervous tension, blend with bergamot. To increase its ability to ease pain, mix with rosemary and lavender.	Avoid during pregnancy. Do ensure that the label reads 'Juniper Berry' and not just 'Juniper'. The latter is an inferior quality oil distilled from the twigs, having an overpowering turpene-like odour.
Lavender (*Lavandula angustifolia*)	Distillation of the flowering tops of the aromatic shrub. The aroma is sweet floral-herbaceous. Its odour effect is uplifting, calming and refreshing.	Skin care (most skin types), respiratory ailments, muscular aches and pains, painful menstruation, headache, depression, insomnia, nervous tension, pre-menstrual syndrome, stress-related disorders.	To support its anti-depressant properties, blend with geranium and neroli or with sandalwood. To reinforce its ability to ease muscular aches and pains, mix with rosemary.	
Neroli (*Citrus aurantium var amara*)	Distillation of the highly fragrant white flowers of the orange tree. The aroma is sweet and floral with a bitter undertone. Its odour effect is uplifting and calming; a reputed aphrodisiac.	Skin care (most skin types), palpitations, poor circulation, pre-menstrual syndrome, depression and other stress-related disorders.	To enhance its stress-reducing properties mix with juniper berry and clary sage. To support its ability to alleviate palpitations, mix with a little rose otto or ylang ylang.	

	Source and descripton	Aromatherapy uses	Blending suggestions	Caution
Rose Otto (*Rose damascena*)	Distillation of the petals. The aroma is sweet and mellow with a hint of cloves. Its odour effect is warming and uplifting; a reputed aphrodisiac.	Skin care (most skin types), respiratory ailments, irregular menstruation, insomnia, headache, pre-menstrual syndrome, nervous tension and other stress-related disorders.	To increase its ability to soothe headaches and promote sleep, blend with lavender. To heighten its sensual properties, mix with sandalwood.	Avoid during the first trimester of pregnancy.
Rosemary (*Rosemarinus officinalis*)	Distillation of the flowering tops of the evergreen shrub. The aroma is camphoraceous with a woody-balsamic undertone. The odour effect is head-clearing, warming and invigorating; a reputed aphrodisiac.	Skin and hair care (oily), respiratory ailments, muscular aches and pains, rheumatism, poor circulation, painful menstruation, colds and flu, headaches, mental fatigue, depression, nervous exhaustion.	To reinforce its invigorating properties, blend with bergamot and geranium. To increase its ability to dispel mental fatigue, mix with a little frankincense.	Avoid during pregnancy. There is also a remote chance that the oil may trigger an epileptic attack in prone subjects.
Sandalwood (*Santalum album*)	Distillation of the roots and heartwood of the tree native to India. The aroma is sweet and mellow with a musky undertone. Its odour effect is relaxing and sensuous; a reputed aphrodisiac.	Skin care (most sky types, especially dry), laryngitis, catarrh, nausea, insomnia, pre-menstrual syndrome, depression and other stress-related disorders.	To increase its ability to loosen catarrh, mix with frankincense or cedarwood. To enhance its anti-depressant properties, blend with bergamot (or a little rose otto) and coriander.	

	Source and descripton	Aromatherapy uses	Blending suggestions	Caution
Ylang Ylang (*Cananga odorata var genuina*)	Distillation of the richly fragrant yellow blooms of the tree native to tropical Asia. The aroma is intensely sweet and floral. The odour effect is warming and intoxicating; a reputed aphrodisiac.	High blood pressure, palpitations, depression, insomnia, pre-menstrual syndrome, nervous tension and other stress-related disorders.	To support its anti-depressant, stress-reducing properties, mix with bergamot and clary sage. To enhance its sensual properties, mix with sandalwood and rose.	

THE HEALING POWER OF TOUCH

Touch is a powerful and natural healing ability that we all possess. When it takes the form of skilled but nurturing massage, not only does it relax and revitalise an ailing or tired body, it is also a way of communicating warmth and reassurance and sense of self-worth. When combined with the mood-enhancing properties of essential oils, we are nurtured on every level of our being, including the intangible spiritual level which may be embraced through our aesthetic appreciation of fragrance.

Although self-massage is highly beneficial (see page 104), it has to be said that receiving massage from someone with 'good hands' feels a great deal better. A professional massage once or twice a month is ideal if you can afford it. Alternatively, you may be able to find another person with whom to exchange massage on a regular basis. By practising on each other, you will begin to develop a sense of how massage should feel, and what feels good to you should also feel good to your partner.

The benefits of massage are far reaching. As well as improving the circulation and alleviating pain and stiffness in muscles and joints, it encourages deep sleep and helps prevent insomnia;

reduces high blood pressure; encourages deeper breathing and is therefore helpful for respiratory ailments and stress. It also triggers the release of 'feel-good' neuro-hormones which in turn stimulate the body's immune defences.

Preparation

Choose a peaceful, well-ventilated but very warm room. It is surprisingly easy to become chilled when deeply relaxed, especially when the skin is coated in massage oil. Chilled muscles contract, causing a release of adrenalin, something you are trying to soothe away in the first place. You can enhance the atmosphere by playing relaxing music at low volume if you wish. If, however, your partner is one of the exceptional few who finds any form of music a distraction, do respect their wishes and turn it off.

Your partner needs to lie on a firm but comfortable surface, such as a couple of folded bath towels or a quilt on the floor. Put a folded towel or cushion under the knees and neck for comfort when your partner lies on their back. When your partner is lying on their front, a small cushion or folded towel under the ankles will add comfort. To ensure that your partner is warm and comfortable throughout the massage, provide extra towels to cover the parts of the body that are not being massaged.

Remember to remove any rings and/or the wrist watch you may be wearing. Likewise, ask your partner to remove any jewellery that may impede the massage. It is also important to ensure that your nails are not too long and likely to scratch your partner

Most important: never give massage while feeling anxious, angry, depressed or irritable. Your partner will pick up your feelings and will begin to feel equally distressed.

Massage Cautions

- Avoid massaging over skin rashes, burns, swellings, varicose veins, areas of broken skin or bruises. In short, if something hurts, abandon the movement and move on to another area of the body.

TIPS FOR GIVING A GOOD MASSAGE

✓ Wear something loose and comfortable and ensure that your hands are warm.

✓ When applying the oil, place a little in the palm of one hand, then rub your hands together to warm the oil. Apply just enough to provide a comfortable slip. Too much oil will cause your hands to slide all over the body part, thus hindering any beneficial firmness of touch. Too little will create uncomfortable friction as a result of dragging the skin. However, certain parts of the body, such as the scalp and feet, can be massaged without the use of oil if you so wish.

✓ Concentrate on the movements, trying not to become side-tracked with idle chatter.

✓ Try to work with the whole of your body. For instance, when kneading, move gently from side to side in time with your hands; when applying the long smooth strokes on the back, lean into the movement, using your body weight rather than just your hands. The more relaxed and fluid your own movements, the more relaxed and at ease your partner will become.

✓ Keep one hand in contact with your partner's body throughout the massage. To break contact mid-flow can feel most disconcerting.

✓ It is also worth remembering that sensitivity combined with the sheer pleasure of giving nurturing massage, no matter how basic, far outweighs a full routine of complicated strokes if they are carried out in a mechanical and impersonal manner.

- Never massage a person who is suffering from a fever or infectious illness. Massage induces heat in the skin, muscles and joints which will exacerbate symptoms.

- Always seek medical approval before massaging anyone with a serious condition such as advanced heart disease or cancer.

- Before massaging a pregnant woman, do seek the go-ahead from the woman's doctor or midwife.

The Massage Oil

A light vegetable base oil such as sweet almond or sunflower seed will help your hands to move freely over the skin. You may wish to enhance the massage by adding a few drops of an appropriate essential oil for your partner's needs (refer to the Aromatic Profiles, pages 85–9). Plant essences are highly concentrated, so they must never be applied neat. The usual concentration is no more than one or two drops of essential oil to every teaspoonful of base oil. As a general guide to quantity, you will need about four or five teaspoonful of base oil for a back massage, and as little as one or two teaspoonsful for the face and neck. Put the vegetable oil into a little dish or saucer, then add the essential oil and stir well.

About the Strokes

The basic strokes you are about to learn can be used to relax or stimulate according to needs. Generally speaking, slow movements are calming; fast movements are bracing. Very slow and deliberate strokes can be erotic – that is to say, if both you and your partner have entered into the massage with Eros in mind. In fact, the power of intent is a vital component of any kind of massage, hence the importance of giving massage with a warm heart.

For the purposes of this book we shall concentrate on massaging the back, head, face, neck, shoulders and feet – areas which tend to harbour a great deal of tension. A good massage (lasting at least ten minutes) to just one part can relax and revitalise the whole person, body and mind. If you would like to learn more about aromatherapy and massage, see the Suggested Reading list.

BACK MASSAGE

approximately 30 minutes

Ask your partner to lie on their front, head to one side, arms relaxed at the sides or loosely bent with the hands at shoulder level. Cover your partner from neck to toe with one or two bath towels. Kneel with your knees slightly apart to one side of your partner.

Attunement

1 Before oiling your hands, move to the left of your partner and place your left hand gently on the back of their head. Place your right hand on the base of the spine. Breathe slowly and deeply, asking your partner to follow your lead so that you are breathing together in unison. Allow yourselves to relax into the experience. Continue for about 30 seconds. This will calm you both and will enable your partner to become accustomed to your touch.

Feathering

(Feathering, as its name suggests, is an extremely light stroke which is barely perceptible to the recipient. Nevertheless it can have a profoundly soothing effect, especially to those suffering from nervous tension or pent-up anger.)

2 Without peeling back the towel, begin feather-light stroking from the top of your partner's head and downwards over the whole body. With hands very relaxed, fingers loosely separated, brush with your fingertips in long sweeping movements from the head to the hips. Take your hands back to the head and sweep downwards again. Repeat at least half a dozen times. Then position yourself further down the body in order to feather from the hips to the feet. Take your hands back to the hips and sweep downwards again, repeating the movement several times.

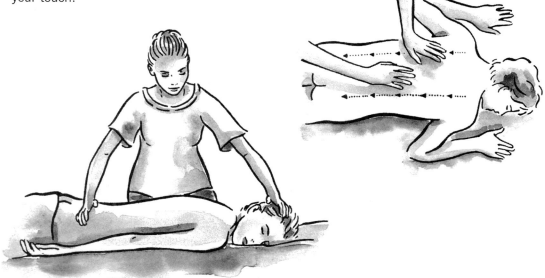

Stroking (effleurage)

(This simple movement is used at the beginning and at the end of a massage, and to ease the flow from one movement to another. You can sit straddling your partner's thighs for this stroke if you wish. Otherwise, kneel to one side of your partner as you did for the feathering strokes.)

3 Peel back the towel, exposing the whole of the back. Begin with your hands at the base of the back, on either side of the spine, with your fingers pointing towards the head. Never apply pressure to the spine itself, but to the strong muscles on either side of the spine. Glide slowly upwards, leaning into the stroke until you reach the neck. Fan out your hands firmly across the shoulders, then glide them down. When you reach the waist, pull up gently and return smoothly to the starting position. Repeat several times.

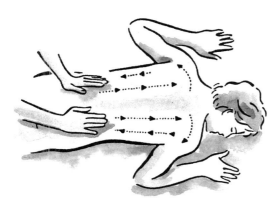

4 Starting with your hands on the lower back as before, glide firmly upwards. When you reach the shoulders, move your hands in circles over the shoulder-blades.

Then continue to make connected circles down the back, until you reach the original position. Repeat several times.

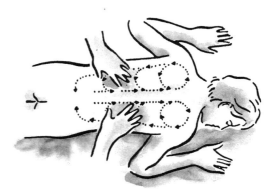

Kneading (petrissage)

(Kneading is carried out on the fleshy muscular parts of the body. It consists of alternately squeezing and releasing handfuls of flesh in a broad circular motion with the heels of the hands and fingers, rather like kneading dough. The same kneading action can also be carried out with just the forefingers and thumbs on small areas, for instance between the shoulder-blades. The purpose of kneading is to relax tense muscles by improving the circulation, and thus the elimination of tissue wastes.)

▶

5 Position yourself to one side of your partner. Starting from the hips or the buttocks, begin to knead. Using the whole of your hands, alternately grasp and squeeze the flesh (but do not pinch).

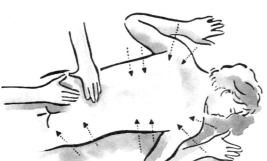

6 Work up the sides of the body and across the upper arms and shoulders, paying special attention to areas of tightness (muscle tension). Move to the other side of the body and repeat.

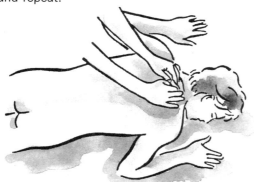

Pulling

(This is a firm lifting stroke used on the sides of the torso.)

7 Remain in position to one side of your partner's back. With your fingers point-ing downwards, gently pull each hand up,

each time overlapping the place where the last hand was. Start at the buttocks and work your way slowly up to the armpits and back down again.

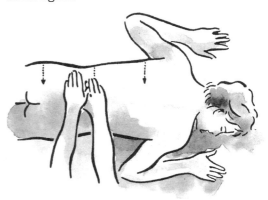

Move to the other side of the body and repeat.

Friction

(The following movements make use of the thumbs to reach deeper into the tissue where hidden tensions lie. Only use friction after you have relaxed your partner's muscles with the previous strokes. You can sit astride your partner's thighs for this stroke if you wish. Otherwise, kneel to one side of your partner at the level of their hips.)

8 Place your hands on the lower back, the thumbs pointing towards each other, on either side of the spine. Keeping your whole hand in contact with your partner's body, lean into the stroke as you glide up the back to the neck. When you reach the top, fan out your hands across the shoulders, ease the pressure and slide them back down to the original position. Repeat two or three times.

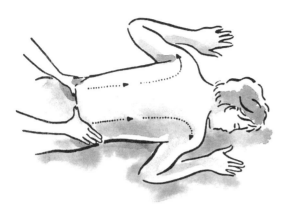

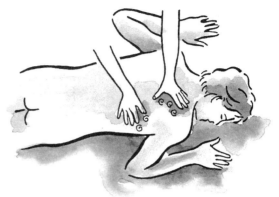

9 Kneel to one side of your partner. Starting from the small of the back, with both thumbs together on the left side of the spine, make small circular movements with your thumbs into the muscles all the way up the spine until you reach the neck.

Soothe the whole back by returning to the effleurage strokes (steps **3** and **4**). Repeat two or three times before moving to the next stroke.

Kneading the neck and shoulders
(Position yourself to one side of your partner and ask them to rest their forehead in their own hands as illustrated.)

11 Using both hands, knead the neck muscles, working up and down the neck to include the muscles at the base of the skull.

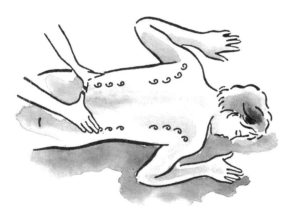

10 With your thumbs on the upper back, continue the circular movements. Work on the muscles above and around the shoulder blades. Then brush your fingertips back down to the base of spine. Repeat the same frictions on the right side of the body.

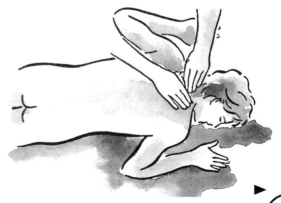

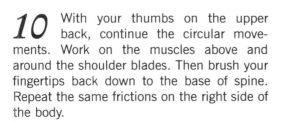

▶

12 Ask your partner to release their hands and place their head to one side as before. Place your right hand on your partner's right shoulder, your left hand on their left shoulder, and begin to knead both shoulders at the same time. Then place both hands on your partner's right shoulder and knead. Repeat the movement on the left shoulder.

Finish the back sequence by returning to the effleurage strokes (step **3**), but this time let the stroking become gradually slower and lighter until you move into the feathering stroke. Repeat several times. When you feel ready, cover your partner's back with a towel. Return to the attunement position with which you began (step **1**). When you feel ready, gently move your hands away.

FACE & SCALP MASSAGE
approximately 15 minutes

A good face and scalp massage can ease away tension and headaches within moments. Only the slightest fingter-tip pressure is required for the face, for it is important not to drag the skin. However, it feels good to receive firm strokes over the scalp.

1 Before oiling your hands, place them on either side of your partner's head, the heels of your hands covering the forehead and your fingers extending downwards, anchoring the sides of the head. Hold them there for a few moments.

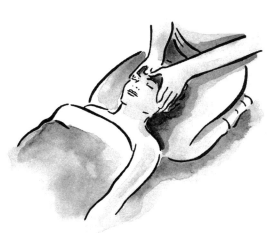

2 Then move your hands to the forehead and smooth the brow hand-over-hand, up and over the hair to the crown of the head.

Move your hands gently away and oil them. You will only need a tiny amount; if you drench the skin, oil is liable to seep into your partner's eyes.

3 Starting from the throat, gently sweep up to the chin, use the whole surface of your hands and slide your hands over your partner's face. Circle the cheeks, moving around the eyes (but not close enough for oil to seep in) and over the forehead. This is to oil the face before you begin the main part of the massage. It can also be used at any time during the sequence to ease the flow from one movement to another.

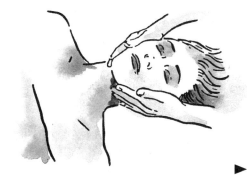

►

The following movements help to release sinus congestion and facial tension.

4 Place the balls of your thumbs at the centre of the forehead between the eyebrows. Slide both thumbs apart and, when you reach the temples, finish with a little circular florish before gliding off at the hairline. Then start a little higher up, sliding your thumbs apart a strip at a time all the way up to the forehead until you reach the hairline.

5 Place the balls of your thumbs at the centre between the eyebrows as before. This time, press your thumbs down quite firmly (your partner will tell you if it is too hard) and hold for about three seconds. Lift your thumbs and place them a little further along the browbone and repeat the pressure. Repeat at intervals until you reach the outer corners of the eyes. Then place your forefingers on the bony ridge *under* the eyes at the inner corners and repeat the pressing movements, a little less heavily this time, until you reach the outer corner.

Then return to the whole face stroking movement described earlier (step **3**).

6 Using your middle fingers, make tiny circles on the cheeks at either side of the nostrils, then over the upper lip and the chin.

7 Place your thumbs on the chin and pull them slowly and firmly outwards and upwards along the jaw-bone to the ear. Then hold the point of the chin between your thumbs and forefingers and squeeze along the whole chin, using a 'milking' action.

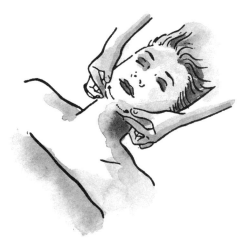

8 Now allow your your partner to bathe in darkness for a few moments. Place your hands gently over the eyes, the heels of your hands creating the darkness, with the fingers extending down over the temples. Keep them there for about half a minute.

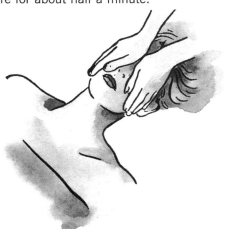

The Scalp

(Unless you wish to apply oil as a pre-wash hair conditioning treatment, there is no need to oil the scalp.)

9 Using your fingers, press quite firmly and move the scalp over the bone. Do not simply slide your fingers through the hair over the scalp. Work up and down the head, covering the whole area. You will also need to place your partner's head gently to the right and then to the left in order to massage the entire skull.

Finish the scalp massage by returning to the holding position with your palms lightly against your partner's forehead with your fingers extending down the temples (step **1**). Hold your hands in this position for a few moments, then gently move away.

─HEAD, NECK AND─ SHOULDER MASSAGE WITHOUT OIL

approximately 15 minutes

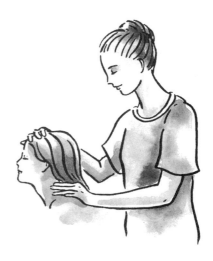

Since there is no need to undress, apply oil – nor even to lie down – this simple sequence can be carried out almost anywhere. Your partner needs to be seated in a comfortable, but upright chair which supports the lower back.

1 Stand behind your partner, then gently place your hands on the crown of the head. Breathe out deeply and allow yourself and your partner to relax into the experience. Hold this position for about 30 seconds.

3 To ease muscle tension and eye strain, hold the head between your hands, fingertips across the forehead. Push gently, first to the left, then to the right, keeping the head straight. Then massage the scalp as described earlier, pressing quite firmly and moving the scalp over the bone.

2 Now place your hands on the top of the shoulders. Begin to relieve tension by kneading the muscles at the base of the neck and across the shoulders. Use small, circular movements with your thumbs. Then place one hand on the crown of the head, while the other hand begins to knead the neck muscles. Start with light kneading and work up to deeper pressure up and down the neck.

4 Then massage the scalp as described on page 99, pressing quite firmly and moving the scalp over the bone. If your partner has sufficient hair, run your fingers through it several times, allowing your fingertips to brush the scalp.

5 Relax the face with gentle feathery movements. Place your palms over your partner's ears and rest your fingers on the cheeks. Then gently brush your fingers upwards from the chin to the crown. Repeat this movement several times.

Finish the sequence by returning to the holding position with which you began (step **1**), before gently moving your hands away.

FOOT MASSAGE

approximately 10 minutes for each foot

The sole of the foot, and also the palm of the hand, contains thousands of nerve-endings with opposite ends located all over the body. For this reason, a good foot massage is a source of great pleasure and relaxation.

As a matter of interest, the popular therapy known as reflexology sees the foot as nothing less than a map of the entire mind/body. Special thumb pressures are applied over the foot (and sometimes the hand) to relieve tension and treat specific ailments. Reflexology is also used as a diagnostic tool. It has been found that pressure applied to a specific reflex point influences the organ or body system to which it corresponds. The lungs, for example, are reflected on the centre of the ball of the foot; the neck, all round the 'waist' of the big toe; the central nervous system, on the centre of the sole, just under the ball of the foot.

Dysfunction in any part of the mind/body will manifest in the foot as crystalline deposits which can be detected under the skin at the corresponding reflex point. The reflexologist works on these deposits in order to disperse them, thus activating the body's own self-healing processes.

However, it is beyond the scope of this book to offer instruction on the art of reflexology; the brief description given above is meant as an interesting aside and an encouragement for further research. Here we shall concentrate on a simple foot massage sequence for soothing away stress. As well as being delightful in its own right – if you do not have

ticklish feet! – the sequence can also be incorporated as a blissful ending to any of the massage routines described earlier.

1 Unless the skin is exceptionally dry, the foot requires very little oil. Before you begin the massage, hold the foot between your hands for a few moments allowing both yourself and your partner to relax into the experience. Then begin to stroke your partner's foot, from the toes towards the body. When you reach the ankles, return your hands to the toes with a light stroke. Repeat several times.

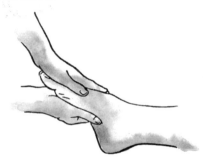

2 Place one hand across the top of the foot at the base of the toes. Make a loose fist with the other hand and position the knuckles just under the ball of the foot. Gently manipulate the foot by pressing and rotating both hands simultaneously in a clockwise direction.

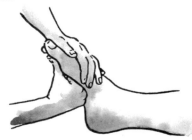

3 Work on the soles of the foot with the thumbs of both hands. Make small circles covering the entire sole.

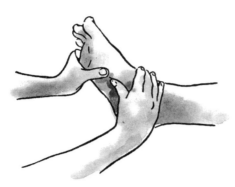

4 Then make thumb circles all over the top of the foot, paying special attention to the area at the base of the toes.

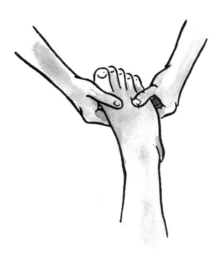

5 Starting with the big toe, gently squeeze and roll each toe between your thumb and index finger; rotate in both directions,

then gently pull them towards you until your thumb and index finger slide off the tip of the toe.

6 To encourage flexibility, clasp all the toes with one hand and bend them gently back and forwards.

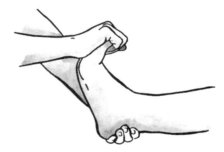

7 Return to the stroking, with which you began, but this time slide your hands very slowly off the end of the toes. Repeat two or three times.

Cover your partner's foot with a towel and repeat the entire sequence on the other foot.

─── SELF-MASSAGE ───

When professional treatment or a willing friend are unavailable, you can still derive much benefit from massaging your own body, preferably with an aromatherapy oil to suit your needs (refer to the Aromatic Profiles on pages 85–9). Self-massage with aromatic oils is a wonderful self-nurturing activity. It is also beneficial for problems such as pre-menstrual tension, mild depression, tiredness or simply for those days when you wake up feeling bad about yourself.

Begin with a bath or shower. The oils will penetrate the skin more readily if it is warm and slightly damp.

The direction of your massage movements should be towards the heart to improve the circulation and thus increase vitality. The only time it is beneficial to massage away from the heart is when you are extremely tense. If this is the case, use very light stroking movements in a downward direction. Generally speaking, however, you should stroke the skin hand-over-hand in an upward direction. Begin with light strokes and gradually let them become firmer and more vigorous.

Once you have improved the circulation by firm stroking, you may begin gently and rhythmically to knead the fleshy areas of your body, such as thighs, calves and buttocks (kneading is described on page 93). You may find it easier to massage your thighs and calves whilst sitting on the floor with your legs bent at the knees to relax the calf muscles.

When you reach your abdomen you may find it easier to massage this area whilst lying down with your legs bent at the knees and feet flat on the floor. Use the whole of your hand and gently circle the area in a clockwise direction. This helps to prevent constipation by strengthening peristalsis (waves of muscular contraction which move food through the intestines).

Sit up and begin to massage your face, neck and scalp. Using the fingertips of both hands together, make gentle circular movements all over your forehead, cheeks, chin, throat and back of the neck. Then massage your scalp as described on page 99. As well as promoting relaxation, regular scalp massage, say, two or three times a week, can help stimulate healthy hair growth by increasing the circulation and thus nourishment to the hair roots.

4

The Healing Power of Nature

*I*BEGIN this chapter with a brief account of my own initiation into the healing power of nature – the discovery that certain places at certain times can be instrumental in bringing about an altered state of awareness. Even though the shift may be slight, the experience is none the less very real and lasting. Most of us have experienced something similiar at least once in our lives, though sadly we may feel obliged to dismiss it as nothing more than a 'flight of fancy'.

THE SPIRIT OF PLACE

It was midsummer when I first awakened to the healing power of nature – a season of almost perpetual light whose influence upon the human psyche is to shorten our natural sleep cycle and enhance dream recall. For many people the mood-altering effects of less sleep, spiced with the quickening scents, sights, tastes and sounds of the Bright Season, triggers a light-headed, almost intoxicated sensation through which we may perceive the world, the rose-tinted highlights of which are almost certain to be recalled on some gloomy winter's day.

Now, sitting by my window gazing at the rain-drenched garden, my mind takes me back to that exceptional summer long ago. I remember as if it were yesterday the school journey by steam train from the murk of London to the mists of Padstow, to the legendary land of Cornwall. Cornwall, the birthplace of King Arthur, so they say, a remnant of Atlantis, or was it Lyonesse? By all accounts, a land of mystery and magic. Certainly the menacing crags, surging ocean and high winds worked strange effects on me – a secret, inner awakening which I could not fully share with my school friends, for there were no words to describe a stirring of the soul by the spirit of place.

Sadly, as is true of most memories of childhood, I have never since been able to recapture the intensity of the original experience. But is such a shift of awareness merely a childish escape into fantasy, a psychological projection or something more than this? Could it be an intermingling with the vital forces of the landscape?

Many traditional cultures throughout the world (including contemporary Japan) allow for the animism of place. The most powerful sites are deemed sacred and include ancient woodland, various mature trees, isolated stones, rocky outcrops, waterfalls, springs, rivers, lakes, streams, seashore, caves, canyons, deserts, mountains and moorland.

While some cultures, at different times, have perceived the spirit of place as a feeling or atmosphere (as in the Latin expression, *genius loci*), others have attributed the phenemonon to the presence of nature spirits. In Greek mythology, such beings were perceived as female and were given generic names: Dryads were the spirits of oak trees; Nereides the spirits of the sea; Oceanides the spirits of the ocean; Naides the spirits of lakes, rivers, streams and springs; and Oreades the spirits of mountains.

With the exception of a handful of visionary theorists like James Lovelock, David Bohm and Rupert Sheldrake, mainstream science is apt to denigrate as superstitious nonsense the whole concept of an animated earth. Even so, the vibrant atmosphere of certain places can be partially explained in scientific terms: as areas of concentrated electromagnetic energy (as detected around standing stones and other quartzite rocks), or places which generate high levels of negative ions (molecules with extra electrons). Negative ions make us feel good. They are especially abundant near waterfalls, and in wild, windy places such as seashore, mountains and moorland.

Whatever the exact nature of this sense of the Otherworld, its doorway is nearly always happened upon rather than arrived at by conscious intent. And when we encounter such realms we cannot fail to be moved by the experience. At such times the 'still small

voice' of the soul may be faintly heard beyond the din of mental chatter, perhaps manifesting as a pleasant, far-away sensation; or as a haunting nostalgia for something indefinable, a sensation which re-emerges just when we thought it had gone for ever. In truth, no life experience is ever forgotten, be it joyful, painful, or apparently of little consequence; it is merely submerged like the sword Excalibur until such time as we are beckoned to recapture its essence.

And just as there are happy places beneficial to well-being, so there are others that seem to harbour sadness or disquiet. The early Gestalt psychologists, Caller and Koffka, believed that the human soul or psyche extended beyond the confines of the brain: that it interconnected with the energies of the outer world. They recognised that a landscape could be happy, sad, exhilarating, soporific, menacing or whatever, because of its expressive qualities (its Gestalt), and not because an emotion has been projected on to it from the subject's innerscape. Although Gestalt therapy is a long way from being accepted by the orthodox world of medicine and psychiatry, its goal is to diminish the gap between the objective and subjective modes of experience, and to restore to a person the validity or 'wholeness' of non-verbal experience (more about this later in Enhancing your Sensory Perception).

There is no need to delve into the intricacies of Gestalt psychology to recognise that, idiosyncractic responses apart, there is a tendency for people to feel somewhat melancholic in still, water-logged places, say, near certain lakes or marshy land. It is also a well-documented fact that people living in low-lying areas (particularly if the land is below sea level) are more likely to suffer from 'cold' ailments such as chronic catarrh and rheumatic aches and pains. But even when wetland is drained to make way for agriculture or the building of homes, offices or factories, many people continue to feel an inexplicable uneasiness about living or working in such areas.

Much also depends, of course, upon the emotional state of the individual perceiving the spirit of place. When suffering from despondency and despair, for example, a landscape which might normally be perceived as peaceful and serene, such as a gently sloping green valley or the inky blue waters of a Scottish loch, may actually intensify depressive feelings. On the other hand, the vibrant atmosphere of high, windy places, such as mountain, moorland and cliff, is more likely to uplift the spirits of the down-hearted. For walking in such terrain almost always bestows far more energy than physically expended.

Yet by law of paradox, places that make us feel sad can some-times be a catalyst for healing, especially where there is a need to release suppressed pain or grief (see also 'Cry Buckets' page 52). Even so, it is important to get the balance right, for dwelling too long in a place of disquiet (not necessarily a sad place) can create a state of chronic disharmony. For instance, it is said that Chicago or 'the windy city' (for it is prone to unusual air currents) was built on ground that the indiginous people call the 'bad lands'. Even though the land had religious significance and certain mystical rites were carried out there, it was not a place where any sane native American would choose to set up home. Little wonder that Chicago was to become the infamous gangland of the 1930s.

Then there is Hollywood. To the native Americans this was the sacred place of dreams and illusion. Today it is the home of the film industry – fantasy and dreams in the making! But is Hollywood a sane place to live?

Without doubt, the indigenous people of the Americas were aware of certain earth energies of which the European oppressers were ignorant, at least on a conscious level. This was a knowledge which was shared by ancient civilizations, and continues to find resonance within traditional cultures throughout the world.

The Artificial Demon of Place

Even without a knowledge of geomancy (earth divination), the detrimental effects upon the human soul of insensitive modern architecture and town planning have become the subject of grow-ing popular concern. As Nigel Pennick, author of *Earth Harmony* puts it: 'The disastrous use of tower blocks for housing, now recognised as dehumanising, came about as a result of the distanc-ing of architects from real human needs and the abandonment of appropriate traditional principles.'

Moreover, where there is socio-economic underprivilege co-existing with aesthetic deprivation there is a higher than average incidence of crime, drug abuse and emotional unrest. It seems that when we develop an urban environment without prior knowledge of geomancy, we run the risk of creating an artificial 'demon of place' – a kind of Frankenstein's monster to which the susceptible become easy prey.

Not everyone, of course, succumbs to the demon of place, even when forced to live in its shadow. We humans have the ability consciously to direct our lives, to rise above such negative influences. More often than not, it is only when we are unconscious of a life-suppressing environment that we become especially susceptible to its lure. Those most at risk are young people who are conditioned into poverty and emotional deprivation. It is a sad fact of life that youngsters who become vandals have a penchant for destroying plants and trees (among other things), especially those planted by local councils in an attempt to ensoul dismal streetscapes. Having made a connection with the demon of place, the ensnared victims are compelled to ravage all that runs counter to the harsh, alienating environment that has become a part of themselves.

Interestingly, the German scientist and philosopher Rudolf Steiner (1861–1925) recognised the importance of nurturing our aesthetic sense through an appreciation of beautiful things in combination with a love of people, animals and nature. If people could be surrounded by beautiful architectural forms, pleasing spaces and greenery, he asserted, crime would diminish. This may have been an overly optimistic assumption, but it is an ideal that modern architects and planners would do well to hold in mind.

SEEKING A BALANCE

While transcendent experience – such as that described at the start of the chapter – may be frustrating to the logical aspect of the mind, to the spiritual aspect of our being it is pure nectar. Yet we need to merge the two aspects of our psyche: the logical 'left brain' with the intuitive 'right brain'. Without this balance, we may on the one hand experience life through a distorted looking glass, without any common or shared basis of reality, or on the other, by shutting ourselves off from other dimensions of awareness, we become impoverished of spirit: quite unable to respond emotionally and philosophically to nature, or indeed to other areas of life.

For example, an overly pragmatic attitude may manifest as cynicism towards anything that could be perceived as being too sentimental, whether it be spotted in the written word, art and music, or in the spheres of business, politics and ideas.

ON COMMUNING WITH NATURE

In an age where the encroachment of 'progress' has never been a greater threat to the very existence of our planet, to extol the virtues of communing with nature is to lay myself open to accusations of blind sentiment or naivety. Indeed, there are those who would argue that we cannot afford to sit back and stare, the provenance of a former age, but that we must rant and rage, wail and mourn and attack those who are responsible for what is happening to the earth.

While I sympathise with this viewpoint, recognising that vandalism does not begin and end in the big city, I also feel there needs to be a balance between fighting and letting go. We cannot allow ourselves to become so distressed that we are unable to respond positively to that which has been conserved (I have met a number of conservationists thus afflicted). To count only what is lost, without also taking into account what is left, is to stifle the existence of joy. And what is life without joy? It is my own belief that to commune with nature not only makes us feel good on a relatively superficial level, but it inspires a profound sense of purpose and meaning to our very existence.

Where does this leave the city dweller who may love the turbulent ocean of bright lights, moving people, multifarious sounds and odours? Or the person who would prefer nature's green cloak, but has little or no choice in the matter? Without realising it, even those people who crave city life can become very much out of balance when cut off from the earth currents. The effects of this may manifest on the one hand as restlessness, insomnia and nervous tension, and on the other, a chronic lack of energy. In either case, emotional disharmony may also be accompanied by a variety of niggling physical ailments which are commonly labelled 'stress related'.

Before we look at some of the ways in which everyone (even

those who can rarely leave the urban environment) may invite nature into their lives, let us consider the position of the confirmed metropolitan. Such a person is apt to ridicule the whole notion of communing with nature in the belief that it lacks sheer excitement. In this sensation-seeking age of horror movies, fast cars, theme parks, electronic virtual reality and chemical highs, nature may indeed seem like a flat option. None the less, even the person who is hopelessly addicted to excitement need not suffer withdrawal symptoms in the presence of nature. Quite apart from pastoral serenity, nature offers active volcanoes, stormy seas, raging torrents and thundering waterfalls. Nature invites exhilarating climbs up lofty mountains, the opportunity to 'shoot the rapids', ride the surf, paraglide, and many other thrills besides!

But what is the catch? Having become as one with the rapid pulse of the wild, the chances are that the 'adrenaline freak' will eventually learn to resonate in harmony with nature's calmer moods. What is more, such a person may even decide to embark upon a wilderness journey – a transformative experience guaranteed to catapult the soul way beyond the shallow waters of the faddish thrill.

THE WILDERNESS EFFECT

The exciting new field of ecopsychology attempts to redefine sanity on a personal and planetary scale. It poses a powerful challenge to the world of psychotherapy whose practitioners tend to practise in an urban environment, in a building which must usually be reached by driving a car along a congested road through a paranoid city. Since mind and nature are inseparable, say the ecopsychologists, a disturbed outer world of nature will inevitably produce a disturbed inner world of the human. And because urban culture itself harbours repressed contents in dire need of cathartic release, how then can it possibly offer a framework for healing the human soul? Indeed, the original place for healing and spiritual transformation was within the midst of wild nature, as far away as possible from urban culture.

The most powerful ecopsychological tool is extended forays (two weeks minimum) into the wilderness. What is meant by wilderness is 'untamed nature' in places such as mountains, forests and deserts: places which have always been used by traditional cultures for healing a troubled soul. Participants on the wilderness trail are encouraged to leave behind the props of the modern world and to enter fully into the experience. Food is carefully planned to be nutritious, but 'just enough'. Only items essential to health and safety are allowed, which means no books, cameras, nor even a pen and writing paper.

The effects of the wilderness experience are profound: 'When we are truly willing to step into the looking glass of nature and contact wilderness', says American ecopsychologist Steve Harper, 'we uncover a wisdom much larger than our small everyday selves.' Although individual experience of the wilderness can be extremely diverse and open to personal interpretation, one of the first things almost everyone experiences is an awakening of the five senses which is a subtly powerful and underrated experience. People discover how greatly our basic modes of perception have been dulled in order to survive the urban world. Participants also speak of feelings of expansion or reconnection. Above all, there is an exquisite sense of aliveness and well-being.

Prior to feelings of exhilaration, however, there is usually a painful transitional period of boredom and depression in which the romanticised idea of 'getting back to nature' is eroded. But once the group has passed through the 'dark night of the soul', amazing things begin to happen. In response to the spirit of the land, twee descriptions like 'picturesque' or 'charming' are wiped clean from the collective vocabulary. There is no longer the sense of beholding a picture, of being an outsider or a visitor. Instead, there is a deep feeling of 'coming home' to wild nature.

Interestingly, when participants were asked to fill out a questionnaire on what they perceived to be the most important part of the wilderness experience, 'alone time' came out on top. This was closely followed by the sheer joy of getting up before dawn and climbing a peak to greet the sun. The third significant aspect was the sense of 'community' or fellowship of the group.

But the real 'personal growth' work begins upon returning to the cultural environment. Initially there may be euphoria as the returned traveller revels in the comforts of modern life. But within a couple of days, positive feelings often dissolve into depression.

Why? In the wilderness the human soul can experience through an 'open' or 'airy' mind. Upon re-entry to the urban culture, however, there is a shocking contrast. The soul is suddenly forced to experience through a 'tight' or 'crowded' mind. There is also the overwhelming realisation that the cultural environment is drastically out of balance – quite mad!

In view of this, it can be tempting to conclude that perhaps it would be better to remain unawakened. However, the purpose of wilderness practice is to 'bring it all back home', to integrate the spiritual into our usual environment. Practitioners of other awareness-expanding methods, such as meditation, yoga, Tai Chi or shamanic dancing, adapt well upon re-entry from the wilderness. This is because they have already learned to extend transformations of consciousness into everyday life.

Another way to buffer the effects of the 'rude awakening' is through sustainable methods of gardening (also organic farming). For as well being a creative balance between wild nature and human nature, there is as much joy in giving to the Earth as there is in reaping her precious gifts.

Moreover, once the self is expanded to encompass the natural world, behaviour leading to destruction of this world will be experienced as self-destruction. Not surprisingly, then, returners from the wilderness almost always become more actively involved (or perhaps involved for the first time) in some aspect of the Green movement.

But is there any real difference between a wilderness trip and a traditional outward bound or adventure holiday? There is indeed a difference – not necessarily in content, but certainly in context. Unlike the average adventure holiday – whose purpose is to meet the challenge of climbing increasingly difficult peaks, or walking for as many hours as possible in a single day – a wilderness trip is not concerned with physical achievement. Rather, it is about rediscovering our primordial wildness (as described earlier), but in a non-competitive way. Since the pace is slow, there is no need to be super-fit in order to join a wilderness group. As British psychologist and wilderness leader Roger Housden explains, 'Often a group will stroll, rather than walk intently . . . Participants just need to be able to walk for a few hours each day and if they weren't fit to begin with, they will probably be so at the end – less because of the demanding schedule than because of the deeper nourishment their being has received.'

If you would like to know more about the wilderness experience, or wish to embark upon a journey with others, see Useful Addresses.

ENHANCING YOUR SENSORY PERCEPTION

We may not need to journey into the wilderness to experience the transformative and healing power of nature. All we need do is develop our ability to look, listen, smell, taste, touch and imagine. In so doing, even the most humble of places – be it the local park or a town garden – may be perceived as wondrous. One way to reawaken the senses is through regular practice of any (or all) of the following awareness-expanding exercises. The ultimate aim of each and every one is to bring the human soul closer to the spirit of Gaia.

Vision

Whether in the countryside, park or garden, focus on a particular plant and observe in minute detail its shape, colour, texture and form. When you feel you have explored every aspect, contrast its mutable hues with the light and shade of the background. Then see your plant in harmony with other plants growing nearby, and with the trees, the slope of a hill, the expanse of the sky. In other words, see your plant in context with everything else – as an aspect of the whole.

What can be gained from this exercise? By learning to apprehend distinctions (in the same manner as the landscape artist) you will develop the ability to see that which was once invisible to you. This means that whenever you happen upon the same species of plant in some other setting, it will magically 'leap out' of the background. This means that a stroll through the woods in springtime, for example, can suddenly take on a whole new meaning, adding untold richness and colour to your aesthetic appreciation of the natural world.

As if this were not enough, neurologists have recently discovered that focused awareness, or 'activation of the attentional mechanisms', causes the formation of new neural pathways in the visual cortex of the brain. This means that it becomes much easier to perceive the intricacies of the natural world, and yet at the same time to apprehend the unity of all things.

(See also Healing Colour Guide, pages 59–60.)

Hearing

Next time it rains heavily, whether you are indoors or outside, close your eyes and listen. Stay with the rainfall for some time, allowing all other thoughts to drift away. If you are indoors, you may be able to position yourself in such a way as to obtain a kind of stereo effect of rain on glass! This is much more likely to occur in a room with a window on two opposite sides, where the right ear may pick up a different rhythm or quality of sound from that of the left.

Should the opportunity present itself, you could also attune to some other form of moving water: a roaring waterfall, bubbling stream, fast flowing river, waves crashing against rocks or rollers gently breaking on the shore.

On a windy day, see if you can find a young tree, no more than 10 to 15 years old, with thin bark and in full leaf. A birch would be ideal. Place your ear against the trunk and you will hear the sap rising up from the roots, compensating for the accelerated loss of moisture through the leaves – a delightful gurgling sound!

At other times, you may enjoy sitting back and listening to the birds, the drone of a bumble bee, a soft breeze rustling through leaves – or to enter into the excitement (or terror) of a sky-cracking thunderstorm!

The benefits of focusing on the sounds of nature are far reaching. In a world permeated with low-level mechanical noise, we easily become conditioned not to notice it at all. That it causes tension, however, is demonstrated by the great relief we feel whenever it suddenly stops. When forced to endure incessant background noise, simply by 'zooming in' on the sounds of nature we can find inner stillness and clarity. Even in the instance of a rip-roaring thunderstorm, peace will come in its wake. It is through the active process of listening, as opposed to the passivity of merely hearing, that the human ear becomes an organ of exalted consciousness.

(See also The Healing Power of Music, pages 27–9.)

Smell

To the sensitive nose, all plants are possessed of some kind of odour. However, the distinctly aromatic plants (those which secrete an essential oil) are highly sensitive to weather conditions, season and time of day. These factors, among others, influence the quantity and quality of a plant's fragrant secretions. With the exception of night-scented flowers like jasmine, nicotiana and honeysuckle, the scents of most aromatics are strongest at midday; though the fragrance of just about any plant is intensified during warm weather, especially after rain. The soil, too, emits a wonderful fragrance when warm and moist.

However, since none of the senses is so easily fatigued than that of smell, you will have to limit yourself to just a few scents per sniffing session. If possible, begin your exploration in a garden full of herbs and fragrant flowers. Failing this, you may be able to obtain a few sprigs of lavender, a richly scented rose, a bunch of fragrant sweet peas or whatever, from a florist, street market or from a friend's garden. Alternatively, you could experiment with a few bottles of pure essential oil; good choices might be lavender, sandalwood and geranium.

Before you begin, breathe slowly and deeply, allowing yourself to relax into a receptive state. When you are ready, inhale the scent of your chosen plant or essential oil. If you are working with an essential oil, never sniff directly from the bottle as the aroma can be overpowering. Instead, put a single drop on to a strip of blotting paper, waft the paper around for a moment to encourage vaporisation, and then inhale the aroma.

Since odour perception occurs mainly in the limbic system or instinctive right hemisphere of the brain, by-passing the intellectual left hemisphere, our response to scent is almost always emotional. A particular fragrance may conjure up a fond memory, pleasing image – a gut-felt 'ugh!' – or something indefinable such as, 'It reminds me of something, but I can't think what'. Next time you smell a fragrant plant or an essential oil, take note of what the scent makes you think of. Is it a feeling, memory or image you would like to have more often?

As you inhale the fragrance, see if you can perceive the ever-changing nuances of aroma. Indeed, the individual scents of nature never resonate on a single odour note, for they are composed of numerous aroma molecules with varying evaporation rates. So the aroma shape-shifts on the air, revealing 'notes within notes'.

It may come as a surprise to learn that it is possible to develop the ability to detect an odour to which we were previously anosmic (unable to smell). For instance, a great many people are anosmic to musky odours, and to scents like sandalwood and freesia which are possessed of a musky element. Odour researchers have shown that people with a total or partial anosmia to sandal-wood, for example, though having a perfectly normal sense of smell in other respects, have been able to generate new olfactory receptors for this particular scent. The secret is to sniff the aroma several times a day for about two months.

Having explored the characteristic odours of individual plants or essential oils, you may wish to delight in a compound of natural scents. One of the most spiritually uplifting ways to perceive the essences of nature is to walk through the wildwood after rain. The scents of wet leaves, earth and wood combine to create an ethereal perfume welcome to the gods!

(See also Healing Aromas, pages 54–8.)

Taste

Taste is an interrelated aspect of smell. For the most part, we need to smell something before we can taste it. So a highly developed sense of smell is synonymous with the ability to enjoy a wide range of both subtle and exotic flavours.

A delightful way to awaken the sense of taste is to ask a friend to join you in a special game. Both you and your partner take it in turns to introduce to the other a cornucopia of tastes. The receptive partner should be blindfolded to enable them to focus on each taste as it is presented. The active partner then proceeds to surprise and tantalise the taste buds of the other with a variety of delectable morsels.

You could perhaps begin with pieces of fresh fruit such as peach, mango, pineapple, grapes or kiwi. Allow a minute or two for your partner to savour the scent, taste and texture of each food before moving on to the next. After the first course, offer something piquant or savoury such as luscious black olives, bits of sun-dried tomato in oil, cubes of cheese or perhaps croutons of bread coated in a favourite dip. Offer the food items on a cocktail stick or small fork. Follow this with sips of red or white wine (or a little of each), fruit juice, sparkling springwater or perhaps iced coffee. If your partner has a sweet tooth, end with a piece of dark chocolate, a mint cream, some vanilla fudge or perhaps a taste of ice-cream.

Yet there is no real need to create such a banquet. As you will discover, even apparently lack-lustre foods like unbuttered whole-meal bread or a plain baked potato can become almost ambrosial when eaten with focused awareness.

Then there is the Epicurean pleasure of going into the country-side and returning with the fruits of nature's store cupboard. In spring we can gather salad greens such as chicory, young dandelion leaves and the cucumber-scented salad burnet. Come summer, and we may find bilberries among the heather, gooseberries in the hedgerows and the sweetest woodland strawberries. In autumn, we can gather hazel nuts, pick blackberries and search for mush-rooms soon after dawn.

To counter any objections to gathering wild food on the grounds that it may encourage further desecration of the natural environment, in *Food For Free* the British naturalist and conserva-tionist Richard Mabey reminds us that:

One of the major problems in conservation today is not how to keep people insulated from nature but how to help them engage more closely with it, so that they can appreciate its value and vulnerability, and, most importantly, the way its needs can be reconciled with those of man. The most complex and intimate relationship which most of us can have with the natural environment is to eat it . . . Far from encouraging rural vandalism, it helps deepen respect for the interdependence of all living things . . . no one is going to stand by whilst the hedge which provides his sloe gin is bulldozed down.

Touch

To enhance the sense of touch, you may enjoy playing a textured version of the taste game described above. This time, include interestingly shaped and textured items such as a piece of driftwood, a sea shell, pine cone, acorn, horse chestnut, smooth pebble, piece of rough quartz, flower petals, crunchy autumn leaf, a fuzz of moss or lichen, feathers, a bowl of sand, your own hair if it is long enough – or anything else you can think of.

As well as putting items in your partner's hand, you might also brush smooth textures against their skin – the lips are especially sensitive. You could also spray the surrounding air (a short distance away from your partner) with some cool water (use a perfume atomiser or plant spray), allowing a fine mist to refresh your partner's skin.

(See also Massage, pages 92–104.)

Imagination

Imagination is fluidity of mind. By entering into a state of perceptual flexibility, you can use your imagination to conjure familiar patterns out of apparent chaos. A cliff wall may take on the features of an ogre; a rocky headland becomes a gaping dragon; the trunk of an ancient oak reveals the wrinkled brow of a druid; and the reflection at the water's edge is a shoal of arrows. Likewise, you can create fantastical forms out of clouds (see Sky Gazing, page 121).

Stretch the imagination a little further, and you may perceive a time-scale way beyond that of a human life-span. For example, as the river meanders from side to side, eroding its banks during its ever-changing course, ox-bow lakes are formed before your eyes. For the river has become a living serpent, weaving its way through the landscape, carving a path to the sea.

By side-stepping our adult sensibilities for just a while, we reconnect with our child-like ability to perceive the natural world as enchanted and alive.

(See also Chapter 6.)

SURRENDERING TO DEPTH

A sojourn into a deep cave can be a healing experience, particularly for people who are either too self-controlled or controlling of others. True, caving can elicit feelings of fearful vulnerability (which is why a great many people refuse to do it), yet the 'closed in' sensation soon gives way to an ecstatic sense of release from having to be in absolute control. The experience of depth also helps us to realise that we are *within* the biosphere – within the body of Gaia – as opposed to being *on* a planet. The latter simply reinforces the mistaken idea that we are separate from the earth.

If the idea of caving sends shivers up your spine, there is another way to bring about a sense of depth, a recognition of being within the earth. Walk through a wild and beautiful steep-sided valley, or along a rocky shore flanked by towering cliffs, and imagine that the trees, boulders, waters, animals and birds are watching over you. If you succeed in entering into the feeling, it will bring about a profound sense of being *part of* and within something much more vast than yourself.

A word of warning: do not apply the same principle in a frantic city, say, whilst walking between towering blocks of concrete, metal and glass. It will only engender a sense of 'Big Brother is watching over me!', or something similarly paranoiac.

SKY GAZING

To engender a sense of freedom, lie on your back and enter into the many moods of the sky. Even in the most built-up areas there is usually a fragment of sky with cloud enough to create meaningful shapes. The most adept shape-shifters are the fleecy piles of fair-weather clouds known as cumulus. Even though it is November, the sky is aglow with such billowy forms. I watch a great polar bear melt into a winged pig; then a boot; then two ragged fish drifting into the blue.

Then there are sunsets. To dissolve into an ocean of crimson marbled with purple and gold is truly wondrous. But what of the dawn? For some reason, our literature is rich in sunsets, but relatively poor in sunrises. None the less, for the determined seeker of the dawn, midsummer is traditionally the most propitious time. As the stars dim, slowly the darkness gives way to a diffusion of gold upon the horizon. Shapes and contrasts emerge from the deep – a furrowed hill, a chimney stack, then a roof top. Yet everything is curiously two-dimensional, like a cardboard cut-out against the sky. Within moments, a tree reveals itself in the quickening light. A bird chirrups – and the morning is born!

At night fall, gaze into the starry firmament. In most cities, the major constellations and the brightest planets, Venus and Mars, are visible on a clear night. In the country, you may even see the Milky Way – a ghostly haze across the sky. After a few months of watching the night sky, it will become apparent that the stars change positions throughout the year (due to the revolving earth), drifting from east to west. In the beginning of your star gazing, however, there is no need to get bogged down with names and positions. Simply enjoy the sensation of free-wheeling into eternity!

Having learned to appreciate the night sky from an emotional perspective, you may decide to give your logical 'left brain' a chance to play. In which case, obtain a good beginners' guide to astronomy and have fun putting names to individual heavenly bodies and star clusters. Moreover, by extending your sight with a pair of strong binoculars – or better still, a small telescope – you will discover that stars come in a wide range of colours, from deep orange through to yellow to bluish-white. The colour of a star depends upon its surface temperature: the coolest stars are reddish, whereas the hottest ones are bluish.

And don't forget to watch the moon. See how she moves across the heavens, rising and setting just like the sun. Unlike the sun, however, the moon will rise in different parts of the sky and at different times. One night you might see her directly above your neighbour's roof, and the next time you look for her, she could be further to the left or the right – or even behind the church at the far end of the road.

Over a period of 28 days, the full moon gradually wanes, disappears completely (the 'dark moon' phase), then grows slowly fuller – rising in daylight and setting in the evening. And so the cycle continues. The lunar cycles pull on the seas and oceans, and the tides of our own body fluids, our moods, our time of receptivity and creativity.

Here is a simple way to recognise the waxing and waning crescents:

The new crescent is cradled in the right hand, the full moon is central, and the dying crescent is cradled in the left hand. Imagine the new crescent as the young girl or maiden, the full moon as mother pregnant with life, and the waning crescent as the old wise woman, decending into the darkness of death, only to rise again. Recognise that your own life can be similarly renewed.

— OTHER WAYS TO EMBRACE NATURE —

● As well as watching for rainbows in the sky, seek them everywhere – in spiders' webs glistening with dew, the mother-of-pearl inside a shell, oil on water, soap suds, a misty waterfall in sunlight, opals, crystals, the scales of a rainbow trout, peacock feathers, the wings of an insect, a prism of glass, even the surface of a gramophone record or compact disk – and in many other glorious and mundane forms.

● Enter into the moods of birds: the movement of wings, characteristic flight patterns, trills and calls, colours and forms. Feel what it is to be 'as free as a bird'.

● The pleasures of sun, sea and sand are well known. Far fewer people, however, choose to swim in rivers, waterfall pools, lakes and lochs. True, such wild and wonderful waters are extremely cold. But, for the hardy among us, they are an invigorating delight. Another option is rain bathing. It sounds eccentric, but should you ever get the opportunity to run naked in the rain (without causing offence to others!) do try it. It will engender a joyous sense of freedom. (See also Air bathing, page 82.)

● Although it is a pleasure available to just a few nowadays, a log fire is one of the greatest joys of life. The brightness, aroma and sheer vitality of a hearth·fire is warming to both body and soul. Living flames also radiate full-spectrum light – important during the winter months when we may be experiencing a degree of light deprivation (see also SAD, page 81). However, if an open fire is totally out of the question in your abode, then perhaps you could indulge in a bonfire somewhere (heeding all the safety precautions, of course). Or how about a camping holiday in the wilds? You will forever cherish memories of sitting around the camp fire, late into the night, gazing up at the stars, staring into the flames – and drifting off into a serene sleep.

● If you are fortunate enough to have a sunny room in your home (particularly if it catches the winter sunshine) a wonderful way to nurture mind, body and spirit is to bask in a sunbeam! First take an aromatic bath or a shower, followed by an aromatherapy self-massage (see page 104). Time of day and weather permitting, place a thick fluffy towel on the floor, in a shaft of sunlight, then lie down and bask for at least 15 minutes. The sensation of warm sun

▶

on your body and the scent of the aromatic oils emanating from your skin is an incredibly sensuous and uplifting experience. Just like the heart-warming effects of a log fire, it will help dispel the winter blues.

● Dispense with electric lighting whenever possible and enjoy the soft, flickering glow of candlelight. During the Dark Season, you could even breakfast by candlelight – the busy (or lazy) person's alternative to early morning meditation!

● Share your home and workplace with as many plants as you can enjoy nurturing. They will literally breathe fresh air into your surroundings (for more, see pages 136–7).

● Make space in your home for natural sculptures such as stones, pebbles, shells, pieces of driftwood, or any other beautiful thing you might find while walking on the seashore, in the countryside or parkland.

● If you have a garden, don't neglect it. Revel in getting your hands dirty in the life-giving soil – and rejoice in watching things grow! (See The Healing Garden, pages 135–7.)

● Most people live in cities, which means our feet rarely touch the earth. Instead, they are cocooned in socks/tights and shoes, and generally subjected to life-suppressing concrete paving slabs, tarmac, vinyl floor coverings, synthetic carpets and such like. Concrete and other artificial materials radiate electrostatic fields which tend to sap our vitality. So give your soles (and soul) a treat! Whenever you can, walk or run barefoot on the beach or through dewy grass. Or simply put on a pair of walking boots and trek over hills and dales, through meadows and woods. The springy turf underfoot will impart a natural bounce to your step, a flexibility that even the most expensive air-cushioned trainers in the world cannot possibly match.

A word of warning to enthusiastic country dwellers intending to 'delight' their city friends: people who rarely leave the urban environment tend to experience difficulty in walking on rough, undulating ground, especially during wet or windy weather. They may trip and stumble over unfamiliar obstacles like tree roots and stones; express concern about getting damp and windswept; or feel most displeased about tramping through mud, cowpats and sheep shit!

TREES

After many centuries of a hack-and-burn mentality towards the forest, humanity is beginning to realise with ever-increasing awareness the importance of trees in relation to the functioning of the ecosphere (the whole planet). Individually and collectively, trees perform many vital roles: they improve the quality of the air we both breathe and pollute; they influence water tables and control floods; they prevent soil erosion; provide habitat for birds and other creatures; temper the effects of potentially damaging winds; they cool streets and buildings; and reduce noise levels.

The pollution-scavenging properties of trees are remarkable. They absorb huge quantities of noxious substances, such as carbon monoxide (the main greenhouse gas), ozone and lead. One study has shown that a tree-lined street may have only 10–15 per cent of the dust particles of a similar street without trees. Since many of the effects of trees upon the ecosphere are still being discovered, the full complexity of their role is far from being fully understood.

Quite apart from their ecological importance, we need trees for their aesthetic qualities: for their beautifying and softening effect upon the landscape, and for their healing influence within the urban environment. A recent study has shown that hospital patients who have a view of trees tend to recover much quicker than those who are totally cut off from nature and this has implications for everyone.

COMMUNING WITH THE SPIRIT OF A TREE

When the native Americans became ill or distressed, one of the first things they did was to enter the forest where they would sit with their back against the trunk of a mature tree. In this way they 'grounded' themselves, 'sitting in the lap of mother' as they put it, to receive healing. Likewise, we too can benefit from this simple practice.

If possible, go out into the countryside and find a mature tree with which you feel a special affinity. The tree may be in the wildwood, a green meadow, on a hilltop – or perhaps in an old churchyard. If you live in a town or city, you may well find a gnarled specimen growing in the local park or a public garden.

Having found your tree, stand beneath it for a while and become fully aware of its presence. Take a deep breath, then exhale with a sigh, letting go of any emotional and physical tension.

Place your hands upon the trunk of the tree and feel the rough texture of its bark. In that roughness there is a soft smile, a gentle smile like that of a loving, weather-beaten father who makes you feel warm and protected. Look up into the green canopy and breathe in the emerald light. Or if it is autumn, delight in the mutable pigments of amber, yellow and red. In winter, find strength in the tree's good bare bones. If your tree happens to be an evergreen, simply revel in its dark greenness.

Now stand with your back against the trunk. Close your eyes and listen to the rustling leaves, a creaking branch, the buzz of an insect, the trill of a songbird – or caw of a crow – and the fluttering of wings as it takes flight. Immerse yourself in the shape – shifting scents of leaves, flowers, fruits or bark – or the earthy fragrance of the crisp brown leaves underfoot. If your tree is a conifer, breathe deeply and absorb the health-giving properties of the resinous vapour. Become aware of your feet and imagine they are just like the roots of the tree, anchoring you to the earth. Now allow your attention to focus on your breath as it flows in and out.

After a short while, you may feel yourself merging with the life-force of the tree. If this sounds abstract, pretentious or simply ridiculous, forgive me. It is almost impossible to describe the feeling, since individual perception varies enormously. However, it is common to perceive an expansive sensation around the head; or there may be a sense that one's body is 'melting' into the trunk of the tree. Some people experience an 'opening' in the chest, or their heart may suddenly miss a beat. Certainly there is no mistaking the moment of connection, for you will experience profound stillness.

When you feel ready, gradually withdraw your consciousness from that of the tree. See that the tree stands before you, quite separate from yourself. Sense its shelter for a moment, before turning and moving away. Before withdrawing, however, you may wish to silently thank the tree for the healing it has bestowed upon you. Or maybe you would prefer to give it a hug!

If this kind of attunement is done regularly, adapting the process to suit your own needs at a given time, vital energy or *prana* will become absorbed into your system and transmuted into a self-healing power.

5 Creating a Healing Environment

*O*UR SENSE of home is infinitely more than the comfort of a roof over our heads. It is a reflection of our inner being. When we invite beauty into our homes, we lavish the same kind of love and attention upon ourselves. Conversely, when we neglect our surroundings, we experience a withdrawal of life-energy. If this sounds unlikely, recall how it feels to arrive home feeling tired and hungry after a long day – only to see the rubbish bin overflowing, the remains of breakfast still on the table and a pile of dirty dishes in the sink!

THE ART OF PLACEMENT

For many people, spring cleaning the home, clearing out clutter and rearranging the furniture is like a breath of fresh air, an auspicious beginning to the Bright Season. But can such changes actually influence our long-term health, happiness and prosperity? For thousands of years this is what the Chinese believed, and feng shui, the art of placement, still thrives in Hong Kong and in variant forms in Bali and Japan. It is now beginning to catch on in the West.

The purpose of feng shui is to design buildings and to arrange furnishings and fittings for the most beneficial flow of chi or life-force energy. Chi flows through our bodies and our surroundings. When the flow becomes impeded, it causes problems such as lack of money, ill health, arguments and unhappiness. When chi is able to flow freely, say the feng shui masters, obstacles – financial, emotional and physical – melt away like snow in the sunshine.

The flow of chi is impeded by such things as clutter, blocked doors, odd-shaped rooms and buildings (L-shaped, for example) and bad siting, like facing the end of a cul-de-sac or a graveyard. 'Cures' for such problems are plants, wind chimes, crystals and, most of all, mirrors. In feng shui, mirrors act to redirect chi along the most favourable routes.

However, even though the fundamental principles of feng shui make good sense, it has to be said that the practice can sometimes fall prey to superstitious nonsense and, worse still, gross materialism. For some people, the almost daily concern about combating 'unlucky spirits' simply adds to their stress. There is also something amoral about the growing number of mega companies and banks employing feng shui experts to help them increase or maintain their already excessive fortunes.

Nevertheless, introducing certain aspects of feng shui can be enjoyable, aesthetically pleasing and genuinely life-enhancing. But it is important to understand that a desired influence is much more likely to manifest if the art of placement is performed with focused intent, not as empty ritual or in a blasé fashion. The power of thought is everything.

Start by spring cleaning your home and clearing out the junk and clutter. Then take a bath or shower and put on some clean clothes. It would also be helpful to sit quietly for a few moments, breathing deeply and allowing physical and emotional tensions to melt away. When you feel ready, make any desirable changes with the help of the ba-gua (see page 130). You may also wish to vaporise 'psychically cleansing' essential oils around the home. The most commonly used essences in this respect are cedarwood, cypress, frankincense, juniper berry, lavender and rosemary. Choose according to your aroma preference.

Other Helpful Influences

- Brighten up a dark corner with a sparklingly clean mirror – the bigger the better.

- Amplify the space of small rooms by introducing mirrors or pictures of landscapes.

- To balance the energies of an L-shaped room, a mirror can be used to make up for the missing chunk.

- Hang bells or wind chimes in the home or garden. They make pleasant sounds which are said to summon up positive chi.

- Cultivate and encourage living things in and around your home – house plants, window boxes, fish tanks, bird feeders, birdbaths.

- Indoor and outdoor fountains are considered highly beneficial, as are ornamental garden pools.

- Bamboo flutes can be played or used for decoration.

- Decorate your home using mood-enhancing tones (see pages 59–60).

- Create a personal sanctuary – especially important if you live with another person who has an overpowering presence. This could take the form of an 'altar', a space decorated with fresh seasonal flowers and floating candles in an attractive water-filled bowl. Just light the candles in the evening for a stunning effect. Otherwise simply place your favourite objects in the space. As well as engendering comforting thoughts, when your eyes rest on such objects self-confidence and self-identity are reinforced.

- Name your home in order to imbue it with personality.

Of course, the art of placement is infinitely more complex than the simple instructions given in this chapter. If you would like to delve more deeply into the subject, there are several good books on the subject (see Suggested Reading).

THE NINE HOUSES OF THE BA-GUA

The ba-gua is an octagonal chart or mystical map on which we can name and relate everything around us. It can be applied to a plot of land, a building or a room to show which areas correspond to specific aspects of your life. The simplest way to begin using the ba-gua is to superimpose it on to a room, aligning the bottom side with the entrance, so that the door falls into the Career section.

The different meanings and symbology of the nine houses are as follows:

Wealth

Can also be called blessings or abundance, as it does not always relate to money. Use beautiful art objects or paintings in this area of your home, especially if they depict palms and willows. The colours associated with this location are blue, purple and red.

Fame

This can mean fame on a public level, but also illumination from within and the ability to inspire others. If you need greater clarity in your life, enhance this area with great poetry, literature or artwork. Or put lighted candles in the space. The most auspicious colour is red.

►

Relationships

Relates to those around you – partner, family, friends and others. This is a good area in which to place happy pictures of you and your partner together. Or use cushions to encourage receptivity. Fortunate colours are red, pink and white.

Family

Concerns your lineage, history and past influences; also relates to bosses and parents. Musical instruments, especially the bamboo flute and upright growing plants are helpful in this location. Green is the most fortunate colour.

Unity or T'ai Chi

This area relates to your health and vitality. Try to keep it uncluttered. A sunflower (or an object depicting sunflowers) would be auspicious in this location. Fortunate colours are yellow, orange and brown.

Offspring

As well as children, this area is associated with personal projects, creativity and change. Enhance this area with aromatic oils, pot pourri or fragrant white blossoms. The most auspicious colour is white.

Knowledge

Relates to introspection and learning – a good place in which to meditate, study or keep your books. Enhance this space with solitary items or empty containers. Helpful colours are black, blue and green.

Career

Your path in life and the way you approach it. In this area of your home place fluid symbols such as a floating candle, silk scarf, sea shells, a bottle of ink or artwork depicting water. The colour black is auspicious in this location.

Helpful People

Help, support and advice from friends, colleagues and officials. Place semi-precious gems or lead crystals here. Since it is equally important to give as well as to receive, positive symbols in this place will also help you develop the gift of empathy. The colours associated with this location are white, grey and black.

REDUCING ELECTROMAGNETIC STRESS

We live in a world that is subject to ever increasing levels of radiation which emanate from high voltage power lines, radio, television, computer screens and so on. It is believed that radiation in its many guises may be responsible for a wide range of illnesses, from fatigue, nervous tension, headache and insomnia to multiple sclerosis (MS) and certain forms of cancer. At the time of writing, there is also suspicion that VDUs may be at least partly responsible for the current increase in male infertility and low sperm count.

Research has also suggested that the prolonged use of VDUs can cause miscarriage or birth defects. Other research, however, offers conflicting evidence. (This is almost certainly due to the idiosyncratic nature of our response to all forms of stress and pollution.) A study of 4,000 pregnant women conducted in the University of Michigan showed that those who work at VDUs for less than 20 hours per week do not increase their risk of miscarriage (birth defects were not mentioned), but that full-time workers show a slight increase in the number of miscarriages.

In view of the risks, no matter how slight, it might be wise for women to give up using the VDU for at least three months before trying to get pregnant.

Generally, if you spend many hours each day in front of a VDU screen, the following advice should prove helpful.

- The desk chair should be comfortable and provide firm support to the lower back. If your feet do not rest flat on the floor, use a foot rest which is high enough to enable your thighs to be parallel to the floor while you are seated.

- Fit an anti-glare filter over the monitor and keep the screen clean and dust free.

- Take breaks every hour or so. Get up, walk around or do some simple stretching exercises. If circumstances allow, the yoga Salute to the Sun sequence is a wonderful revitalizer (see pages 78–80).

- To help prevent RSI (repetitive strain injury), massage your hands, fingers and forearms at intervals throughout the day.

Fortunately, most people are able to adapt to a certain degree of radiation, including that which in some people causes 'geopathic stress' – the effects on the mind/body complex of natural radiation coming up from underground streams or from granite. Yet there are those experts who would argue that although the human organism has learned to adapt to natural sources of radiation, that which emanates from high-tech devices is somewhat different and therefore potentially more hazardous.

British scientist Dr Mike Adams has discovered the radiation-blocking powers of clear, unpolished quartz crystals. A large crystal, say 7–10 cm long and about 4 cm wide, can be placed close to the mains fuse-box. This acts to prevent power socket radiation (which can sap the vitality of certain individuals) from going beyond that point. Similarly, small quartz crystals can be placed on and around televisions, microwave ovens and computer terminals to help 'fight back' the radiation (see also the information on the Column Cactus, page 136).

Believe it or not, however, some people become addicted to radiation! Dr Adams warns that during the first week of using crystals as an anti-radiation measure, some people suffer worsening of symptoms – though he assures us that withdrawal symptoms are temporary and harmless, and may be alleviated by a tot of whisky or a glass of champagne! He also suggests the more modestly priced Bach Rescue Remedy (see page 41).

Health Benefits of Indoor Plants

House plants are not only pleasing to the eye, they are positively good to have around. Some well-nurtured specimens will increase oxygen levels in the home, improve humidity and literally raise the vibrations of a space by generating revitalising negative ions.

Experiments carried out by NASA (North American Space Agency) concluded that certain plants can filter out common air pollutants such as benzene, carbon monoxide, trichloroethylene and formaldehyde which are found in products as diverse as foam insulation, carpets, furniture, cigarette smoke and paint fumes.

Other Ways to De-Stress Your Home

- Air rooms by opening the windows for a minimum of 30 minutes every day – even during the winter months.

- Use ionisers around the home to compensate for excessive positive ions generated by electrical equipment. However, it is essential that the ionising equipment you choose is properly insulated. Unfortunately, most ionisers are not and they produce high electromagnetic fields which are therefore counter-productive. Recommended models are made by Mountain Breeze.

- As an alternative to the ioniser, put a bowl of water in the room as this helps absorb positive ions. It will also act as an humidifier – important during the winter months when the heating is on high and the windows tightly shut.

- When watching television, sit at least 6 ft away from it. The larger the screen, the wider the electromagnetic fields.

- Keep electrical equipment in bedrooms to the bare minimum. If you feel your sleep patterns are being disturbed by electromagnetic waves, turn off your mains switch at night. It is also important to avoid sleeping directly above or against the same wall as the mains electricity box. Electromagnetic fields can pass through walls, floors and ceilings.

- Use natural materials such as wool, hessian and cotton for carpeting whenever possible.

- Avoid synthetic furnishings, bedding and clothing whenever possible.

- Avoid cooking with a microwave. Older models can leak radiation, though microwaves of any age should be checked regularly, especially if you suspect the door is ill-fitting or has been damaged.

- Vaporise essential oils such as cedarwood, lavender, bergamot, peppermint, pine, eucalyptus, tea tree, lemongrass and rosemary. As well as repelling insects, these particular essences are powerful slayers of air-borne microbes – and they smell good too. (Instructions for vaporising essential oils are to be found on page 56.)

NATURE'S POLLUTION BUSTERS

Some plants are more effective at absorbing toxic gases than others, but in general, the removal rate ranges from 10 to 90 per cent, averaging at around 60 per cent. It is also important to mention that plants are more likely to stay healthy if they are grouped together, for this increases the humidity of the air around them.

Pollutant	Potential health risks	Plant aid
Formaldehyde The major sources are foam insulation, modern sofas and armchairs, carpets, floor coverings, tissues and cleaning agents. It can also be found in cigarette smoke and mains gas.	Irritation of mucous membranes of the eyes, nose and throat. May also cause skin rashes. 	Spider plant: (*Chlorophytum elatum*); Sweetheart Plant (*Philodendron scandens*); Golden Pothos (*Scindapsus aureus*): Azalea (*Rhododendron indicum*); Poinsettia (*Euphorbia pulcherrima*); Dumb Cane (*Dieffenbachia masculata*); Chrysanthemum; Mother-in-Law's-Tongue (*Sansevieria laurentii*).
Benzene A commonly used solvent also present in petrol, ink, oil, paint, plastic and rubber. It is also used in the manufacture of detergents, pharmaceuticals and dyes.	Irritation of eyes and skin, headaches, drowsiness, nervousness, loss of appetite.	English Ivy (*Hedera helix*); Dracaena (*D. marginata*); Janet Graig (*D. deremensis*); 'Warneckei' Peace Lily (*Spathiphyllum*); Chinese Evergreen (*Aglaonema*); Mother-in-Law's-Tongue (*Sansevieria laurentii*); Fig Tree (*Ficus moraceae*).
Trichloroethylene Widely used as a degreaser and dry-cleaning fluid. Also used in paints, inks, lacquers, varnishes and adhesives.	A potential liver carcinogen (cancer-inducing agent).	Chrysanthemum; Peace Lily (*Spathiphyllum*); (*Dracaena deremensis*) 'Warneckei'.

▶

Pollutant	Potential health risks	Plant aid
Electro-magnetic fields (EMFs) Generated by electrical equipment (VDUs are especially problematic), electricity meters, power sockets and cables.	Weakened immunity, headaches, depression, fatigue, irritability, menstrual disorders, infertility, miscarriage, skin rashes, eye disorders and more.	The Column Cactus (*Cereus peruvianus*) is believed to be effective at neutralizing the harmful effects of VDU emanations. A large specimen (at least 8 in tall) should be sited close to the computer.

When such noxious substances are allowed to accumulate (as a result of super-efficient insulation) they can contribute to a blocked nose, itchy eyes, skin and respiratory ailments, stomach ache, headaches and devitalisation.

A growing number of researchers like Dr Bill Wolverton (formerly of NASA) are focusing their attention on combating the problem of 'sick building' syndrome. This occurs when a building has no fresh air and is badly designed. People living and working in sick buildings tend to develop symptoms such as those just mentioned. The remedy, claims Dr Wolverton, is to place a variety of plants around the office and home, for this will greatly improve air quality. See chart on pages above for specific advice.)

How exactly do plants remove pollutants from the air? The magic lies in plant metabolism. Plants require a continuous exchange of gases (usually carbon dioxide, oxygen and water vapour). Research has shown that plant leaves and roots can absorb high levels of other gases – substances which are toxic to humans – and synthesise them into nutrients. The effectiveness of a plant's recycling system is increased when it is exposed to contaminants over a long period, that is to say, months rather than days. So, although a plant would prefer to thrive on a balanced diet of natural gases, it can if necessary survive on a diet of 'junk' air.

THE HEALING GARDEN

While the wilderness provides its own form of healing magic, the garden is a tamed place of the soul, a sanctuary in which we may work with the forces of nature, and in accord with the spirit of the land. It is a place in which we may receive nourishment for our physical and emotional well-being.

So if you have a garden or a back yard, no matter how small, do not neglect it. Any amount of effort will be richly rewarded, and not just in reaping the fruits of your labours. As every gardener will tell you, there is something primordial and deeply satisfying about working the land, a feeling that can only be experienced rather than explained. Of course, growing things in pots and window boxes is immensely satisfying too.

In view of my own field of work, this section would not be complete without offering a few hints on creating a garden of fragrance. Just as you learned to blend mood-enhancing room scents using essential oils, you can create an ethereal garden whose individual scents merge into a veritable symphony of fragrance. And when you move through the garden you will instinctively breathe more deeply in order to experience the scent fully – and the more deeply you breathe, the more relaxed and in harmony you will feel.

According to botanists, however, our enjoyment of fragrance is *incidental* to the reason why plants produce scent (the main function of which is to attract pollinating insects). Yet it is also said that nothing in nature is without a purpose, and that everything in the ecosystem functions as an interrelated aspect of the whole – albeit humans have the capacity to fight against nature. But we cannot survive without eating plants (or the animals that live off plants) and breathing in the oxygen they produce. Likewise, the human spirit is nurtured through our sense of the aesthetic – especially our appreciation of the fragrant earth.

If you are fortunate enough to have a garden, the following tips may help in creating a perfumed haven with two distinctly different themes: a secluded garden of tranquillity and an open garden of frivolity. Of course, the flowers suggested here can only be a rough guide because you will need to discover which plants are suitable for your own garden with its idiosyncratic features, soil quality, climatic conditions and available space. A good gardening book is essential (see Recommended Reading).

Garden of Tranquillity

Create this in a secluded spot in a quiet corner of the garden, per-haps with a seat surrounded by soft foliage plants and gently arch-ing branches where you can simply sit and stare. Ideally, there will also be pool of still water – a focal point for contemplation and reflection.

Even though many fragrant plants need to be grown in full sun, there are some exceptions, one spectacular example being the love-ly night-scented nicotiana or tobacco plant which will emanate a heady perfume if grown in semi-shade. If you wish to experience a wider variety of fragrance, ensure that the garden seat is positioned in such a way as to allow you to see and smell other scented plants growing in a sunny spot nearby.

When choosing fragrant plants, it is necessary to 'play it by nose'. While some people find the warm and intoxicating scents of honeysuckle, jasmine and white lilies sedating, others find such perfumes overpowering and even nauseating if inhaled for too long. Even if you are relaxed by richly scented blooms, you could perhaps compromise to enable others of a weaker constitution to enjoy the area as well. If this is the case, opt for light, airy fra-grances such as lavender, bluebells and softly scented roses. But what about colour?

We saw in Chapter 2 that green is the colour that helps to allay anxiety and brings about peace and well-being. Since green is the predominant colour of nature, it is no wonder that she can bestow tranquillity to the frenzied and uplift the spirits of the downhearted.

When seeking to capture serenity, the creative gardener is drawn to plants whose colours, shapes and scents whisper but never shout. So the planting scheme most conducive to relaxation is one which emphasises cooling blues and purples, perhaps with a tinge of rose-pink to warm the heart, and a drift of white or cream to ele-vate mood. Unscented foliage plants such as ferns and ivy, and also delicately painted flowers like larkspur, campanula, love-in-a-mist and columbine have a place too, as does the curiously beautiful passion flower. Any of these can be incorporated to enhance colour and form.

Garden of Frivolity

This needs to be created in a sunny part of the garden; a riot of colour planted in a free-spirit style. It can be a place to go when you need to be revitalised. Ideally, there will be a bubbling fountain – a focal point for generating energy.

Choose brightly coloured flowers whose scents are spicy, citrus or sweet and light-hearted. A good choice is dianthus (the garden pink) whose colours range from pale pink to deep red. The blooms have a warm scent with a spicy nuance reminiscent of cloves. Other plants, like lemon balm, lemon geranium and rose geranium have deliciously fragrant leaves which release their scent molecules in hot sunshine, or whenever you brush past them. If you have enough space the golden flowered azalea is a must. Its exotic fragrances suggest the essential oil of ylang ylang, albeit more airy and less intensely sweet.

No garden of frivolity would be complete without a few raucous annuals. Even though most have little or no scent (at least to the human olfactory sense), they can impart a sense of abandoned rapture. The rampant nasturtium is one of my own favourites. If left unchecked it will trail-blaze through the garden and beyond, providing a cornucopia of orange-red blooms from early summer until late autumn. As a bonus, the leaves, flowers and seeds can be used in salads for novelty – and to catch the uninitiated by surprise with a peppery kick! Then there is the lovely pot marigold whose faint dry fragrance can be detected if the blooms are sniffed close-up. And if you have room, the 'dwarf' multi-headed sunflower (reaching up to 5 ft) will add a certain leonine charm.

Some Highly-Scented Plants

Azalea
(*Rhododendron leteum*)
A small shrub producing clusters of golden yellow flowers in the spring. The heady perfume wafts for many yards.

Daphne
(*Daphne mezereum*)
A small flowering shrub producing an abundance of sweetly fragrant purple-pink flowers during late winter and early spring.

Dianthus
(*D. caryophyllus*) variety 'Mrs Sinkins'
A delightful plant related to the carnation. The white clove-scented flowers appear from early summer onwards.

Heliotrope
(*Heliotropium peruvianum*)
The purple or white flowers emanate an unusual fragrance reminiscent of cooked cherries and almond. Blooms midsummer.

Honeysuckle
(*Lonicera periclymenum*)
A hardy rambler which produces masses of tubular creamy yellow flowers for most of the summer and autumn. The scent is intensely sweet and intoxicating, especially in the evening.

Jasmine
(*Jasminum officinale*)
A rambling plant producing an abundance of night-scented white blossoms which appear from late summer to autumn.

The heady perfume is divine, at least for those with a penchant for overtly erogenic scents!

Mignonette
(*Reseda odorata*)
Although the clusters of small yellow flowers are not particularly attractive, their voluptuous perfume more than compensates for their modest appearance. Indeed, the perfume is almost drug-like in its strength! Blooms midsummer onwards.

Nicotiana or Tobacco Plant
(*N. alata*)
A night-scented plant with loose clusters of white tubular blooms which appear from midsummer until the first frosts. The perfume is intoxicatingly sweet with a nuance of nutmeg.

Rose
(*Rosa gallica officinalis*) variety 'Belle de Crecy'
A beautiful shrub rose producing double flowers, almost magenta coloured, changing to violet. Blooms throughout the summer. The rich, velvety scent is truly superb.

Sweet pea
(*Lathyrus odoratus*) variety 'Charlie's Angel'
A delicately painted climber with a penetrating sweet-spicy scent. The flowers of this particular variety are blue and lavender and appear from midsummer onwards.

Wallflower

(*Cheiranthus*) variety 'Orange Queen'
The velvety orange-brown petals emanate a beautiful sweet-spicy scent from spring to early summer.

The Art of Creative Imagery

6

*I*MAGINE being able to take off for some paradisaical place whenever the fancy takes you. Imagine it now – and you are there! Indeed, current biofeedback research into the efficacy of creative imagery has proven without doubt that simply imagining ourselves in a warm nurturing situation has the same effect as actually being there. For some this place might be a sun-drenched beach, for others a beautiful garden. Wherever the place may be, the focus is on making the image as real as possible.

THE BENEFITS OF CREATIVE IMAGERY

The benefits of imagery work can be far reaching; by enabling us to communicate with the deep psyche, it reduces stress levels, strengthens our immune defences, hastens recovery from illness and promotes personal happiness.

The most remarkable work carried out in this field was initiated by Carl and Stephanie Simonton, at the Cancer Counselling and Research Center in Fort Worth, Texas. Cancer patients were taught how to achieve a state of deep physical relaxation, followed by a series of mental pictures of the cancer cells being destroyed in their body. While one person may choose to conjure up a golden vacuum cleaner which goes around the body sucking up cancer cells, a different individual might imagine an amoeba that quietly engulfs the rogue cells. So long as the image is compatible with the individual concerned, and is geared towards destroying cancer and restoring health, it does not matter what exactly it is.

The Simontons found that such images helped to bring about remissions and sometimes complete recovery. In one particular case, a 61-year-old man who had been advised to practise an imaging exercise several times a day not only overcame his cancer, but also rid himself of arthritis and impotence which had plagued him for more than 20 years!

Creative imagery is also increasingly being employed for improving health and a sense of well-being in those who show no obvious signs of illness. Then there are those who use the technique to enable them to achieve a desired goal or change that is actively being worked towards. This can be anything from giving up smoking, increasing athletic performance through to inner changes in psychological response or emotional patterns.

However, it is advisable to receive expert instruction and guidance in the use of imagery work for specific health and/or emotional problems at first, as there are pitfalls for the unsuspecting novice. It can be all too easy to programme in the wrong thing. Clinical hypnotherapists or psychotherapists experienced in the use of imagery are excellent people from whom to learn the necessary techniques. You will also be given assistance in developing appropriate and personalised suggestions.

What about self-improvement tapes? Excellent as many of these are, unfortunately there are also some badly produced and potentially harmful productions being sold to an unsuspecting public. It would seem that the sole aim of some of these tapes is to prey on the insecurities of the vulnerable – and to fatten the wallets of those who produce and market them. One catalogue of 'self-empowerment' cassettes, for example, promises that you can: 'lose weight and be happy'; 'become devastatingly attractive to the opposite sex'; 'enhance the shape and size of your breasts'; 'become a money magnet'; 'stay young for ever'; 'transcend the wheel of karma'; and much more besides.

True, there are those who would swear that they have effected such changes as a result of using these tapes. But this is not the real issue. Anyone who has deep-rooted insecurities is likely to feel even worse about themselves should they fail to achieve what they desire through the creative imagination. At risk of sounding trite, a great many people who collect such tapes (and indeed books on the same subject) are in desperate need of the healing power of Love – an elusive gift in this present era of over-ambition, fear of the ageing process, gross materialism and chronic unrest.

Therefore, the guided imagery work suggested in this chapter is not aimed at changing anything in particular, nor is it about creating material wealth. On the contrary, it is about taking time out from such stress-inducing pursuits. But what can we hope to receive in return for our efforts? A truly magical gift – the ability to tap into our own inner source of peace, healing and wisdom.

Before going any further, an important point must be made here about the term 'visualisation', which is often regarded as synonymous with 'imagery'. Visualisation is an important, but specific aspect of imagery. Studies have shown that the form of imagery which most powerfully connects with the deeper levels of the psyche involves all of the senses. In addition to visualising or 'seeing' a beautiful garden, for instance, the aim should be to feel it, smell it, hear it, and even taste it. We might touch the bark of a tree, perceive the scent of roses, the song of a bird, and the taste of a sun-warmed strawberry. Kinesthetic evocation is important too – the sense through which we are aware of the body and its movements.

No doubt, you will discover that one or two of your senses are more highly developed than the others. For most people, visual imagery is the easiest to evoke: odours the most difficult. A person's occupation, however, will exert an enormous influence upon their sensory development. While the perfumier or aromatherapist, for example, will have little trouble imaging specific aromas, the musician will have a more highly developed ability to conjure up sounds. For the chef, the senses of taste and smell will be equally developed; and for the dancer or athlete, kinesthetic awareness will be especially acute.

Once you have perfected the sensory evocation exercises opposite, you will be ready to explore the art of guided imagery. Incidentally, mastery of the exercises can take anything from one or two practice sessions through to many sessions over a period of months – depending upon the flexibility of your imagination. Indeed, the imagination, just like our muscles, becomes more powerful and limber through frequent use.

SENSORY EVOCATION EXERCISES

Sit comfortably in a quiet room, either cross legged on the floor if you are used to this position, or in an upright chair which supports your back. Close your eyes, breathe out deeply with a sigh, allowing all the cares of the day to melt away. When you are ready, try to visualise the following.

- A pen slowly writing your name on paper.
- An azure sky with billowy clouds floating by.
- Various coloured shapes: a red triangle, a yellow circle, a blue square, a green five-pointed star, and so on.

Now focus on the sensation of touch.

- Stroke a cat or a dog; feel the texture of its coat and its warm body.
- Put your hand in a bubbling fountain and experience the sensation of cool water dancing on your skin.
- Pick up a pine cone and feel its rough multi-layered form.
- Stroke a feather.
- Roll an orange in your hands, feeling the dimpled texture of the rind.

Imagine the flavour, temperature and texture of:

- vanilla ice-cream
- marzipan
- strawberries and cream
- a piece of dark chocolate
- black olives
- avocado.

Then try to conjure up the following aromas:

- your favourite perfume or essential oil
- wood smoke
- seaweed
- freshly baked bread
- coffee
- peppermint.

In your mind's ear, listen to the following sounds.

- Waves breaking on the sea shore.
- Children's voices in a school playground.
- A voice calling your name.
- Birdsong.
- Raindrops tapping against a window.
- The drone of a bee.
- Autumn leaves crunching underfoot.
- The sound of a gong, gradually fading into silence.

And finally, the kinesthetic sense. Imagine that you are doing the following.

- Swimming; experience the sensation of weightlessness as your body glides through the water.
- Dancing; feel the rhythm of the dance throughout your body.
- Walking then running along a beach; feel every movement of your muscles.
- Digging the garden or chopping wood.
- Moving to and fro on a garden swing.
- Moving back and forth in a rocking chair.

CREATING AN INNER SANCTUARY

This is a wonderful exercise for just about everyone, but especially those who lead extremely busy lives and who rarely have the opportunity to experience nature at first-hand. The secret garden sequence given below is one of my own favourite places of the soul. However, your own idea of a nurturing place may be quite different. It could be the sea shore, a green valley, a pine forest, the desert, a secret place in the mountains – even a fantasy setting in some other world – or it could be a beautiful place you have actually visited.

By all means, work with the secret garden sequence if it feels right for you. Otherwise, allow a magical sanctuary of your own choosing to form in your mind's eye. Find an idyllic place in nature where you can relax and enjoy yourself, knowing that there will not be anyone else there unless you invite them.

When creating your own guided imagery sequence, here are a few guidelines.

- As a preliminary to guided imagery work, it is important to ensure that you are completely relaxed by working through the conscious relaxation sequence described on pages 20–1.

- When actually employing imagery, try to bring all of your senses into play. What can you see around you? What is on the ground? And what does the ground feel like underfoot? Is the air warm, cool, moist, dry or breezy? Are there any scents wafting on the air? And when you look up, what does the sky look like? What sounds can you hear? What can you taste? Can you sense the movement in your limbs as you wander through your inner sanctuary?

- Always begin and end your journey in exactly the same place as this imparts a sense of completeness.

- At the end of the sequence, say farewell to your inner sanctuary, but remind yourself that you can return any time you wish. It is always there for you whenever you need to relax, to be by yourself, and to be nourished spiritually.

You may wish to record your guided imagery sequence on to tape, with appropriate pauses and soft voice. Otherwise, work with a sympathetic friend or partner, someone with whom you can exchange the roles of narrator and explorer. Of course, guided imagery tapes on the 'inner sanctuary' theme are commercially available, but it can be difficult finding a recording that captures your own personal idea of a spiritually uplifting place. Should you choose to work with the following sequence, do feel free to alter it here and there to suit your own sense of harmony.

THE SECRET GARDEN

Ensure that you will not be disturbed for at least half an hour. Avoid the use of background music and room scents as they may intrude upon your ability to image the sounds and scents suggested in the sequence. If you are unable to record the narrative, read it through a number of times until you can summon to mind the various stages without having actually to read the text. Immediately before you begin the sequence, it is important to spend at least 15 minutes relaxing your body and mind as described on pages 20–1.

Imagine you are walking along a path through a wide green swathe. It is a warm, sunny afternoon and there is a gentle breeze carrying the scent of new mown hay. The path leads to a weathered oaken door, partially obscured by overhanging ivy. You move aside the swinging curtain of green and push back the door which opens slowly. You catch your breath in sheer wonder and delight, for you are standing in a walled garden of immense size and beauty.

Before you is an abundance of rambling roses clambering over a wooden pergola. The dark red velvety blooms emanate an exquisite perfume. You breathe a little deeper in order to enjoy the fragrance. A soft wind scatters the fallen rose petals about your feet, imparting a sense of abandoned rapture. In a curved flower bed nearby are tall blooms of a sapphire hue, rising above floral clouds of pink, purple and white. Aromatic herbs fill the gaps between stepping stones, and ferns push through cracks in the grey stone wall. Everywhere you look, flowers, shrubs and foliage plants grow up in luxuriance and profusion.

You follow some stepping stones which lead through the pergola walkway and meander down to a wildwood area of the garden. On entering the copse, you pause for a moment to run your fingers over an aged bronze sculpture of a seated girl, finding it cool and dimpled to the touch. You breathe more deeply in order to enjoy the sensation of the damp woodland air

▶

and earthy scents. Throughout the copse, the tall, bright, tender grass is bejewelled with wild flowers: some flushed pink, some tinged purple, and some like brilliant white stars. Looking up, you see wild clematis and honeysuckle creeping from tree to tree, hanging from branches and forming light, swaying curtains, some making wonderful arches of themselves.

Moving through a leafy arcade, you hear the fluttering of wings. A song thrush perches high in a tree: his jubilant song echoes through the greenwood. A fluty call that seems impossibly loud for so small an instrument.

Continuing on for a short while, you reach the edge of the copse. Growing on a bank in dappled sunlight are clusters of tiny wild strawberries, looking delicately vivacious with their three-fold leaves and clear white blossoms. You are tempted to pluck a fragrant sun-warmed berry. Popping the fruit in your mouth, you savour its sweetness.

On emerging from the green shades, you feel the warm sunshine on your face and bare arms. An emerald carpet of soft grass is laid out before you, inviting your feet to move freely over it. And indeed the springy turf imparts a sense of freedom to your step. After walking a short distance, you come to an evergreen hedge with an archway fashioned through it. Looking through the arch, you see a perfectly straight path, bordered on either side by brightly painted flowers, leading to a cascading fountain. The dancing waters beckon you to their source. On reaching the fountain, you sit on its curved stone edge. A fine mist spray refreshes your face. You dip your hand into the sparkling pool, gliding it to and fro, enjoying the tingly sensation of energised water moving through your fingers.

A darting dragon-fly suddenly lands by the fountain's brink, capturing your attention with its iridescent beauty. Fiery with purposeful energy it takes off again, flashing electric blue as it disappears over the hedge. You sit a little longer, gazing up at the summer sky, watching fluffy white clouds drifting by – and listening to the song of tumbling water . . .

And now the time has come to say farewell to your secret garden, at least for the time being, but you know you will soon return. Gradually, you arise and make your way back through the gardens and the wildwood, out through the oaken door, which you remember to close behind you, along the path through the green swathe, and into everyday reality. You feel wonderfully alive and joyful – ready to take on the world!

Now take a couple of slow, deep breaths, then raise your arms overhead and have a really good stretch from fingertips to toes. When you feel ready, roll over to one side before slowly getting up.

7

Devising Your Own Life-Enhancing Programme

*I*F YOU have read everything so far, or at least skimmed through the chapters, you may be wondering how to begin putting it all into practice. In fact, it is not expected that you should carry out everything suggested in these pages; rather, you are encouraged to choose those things which you know will sustain your interest. Remember, body, mind and spirit are interrelated; whatever affects one aspect – the body, mind or spirit – affects the *whole*. So should anything become a chore, its effects will be counter-productive: radiating subtle stress waves throughout your whole being.

Nevertheless, no serious stress-reducing and health maintenance plan would be complete without some attention to the following elements: nutrition, breathing, movement, relaxation. In practical terms, this involves eating a varied wholefood diet, practising the yoga complete breath, taking a brisk half-hour walk every day and allowing time in your daily routine for some form of nurturing, creative or frivolous activity – something which enables you to completely unwind. This can be anything that gives you pleasure, say, putting your feet up with a nice cup of tea, playing with the children, having a long soak in the bath, reading your favourite magazine, putting on some uplifting music, or simply listening to the birds. Having taken care of the basics, you may wish to include other life-enhancing practices such as conscious relaxation, meditation, aromatherapy, colour work, nature attunements and creative imagery.

'That's all very well, but I really don't have time!' If this frustrated remark mirrors your own perspective, then read on . . .

ORGANISING YOUR TIME

Even though everyone would agree that there are 24 hours in a day, it is also true that time is malleable, depending upon our own individual perspective. For some people, time is a rationed commodity, and so they are constantly rushing about, frequently late and forever trying to cram more and more things into the day. Then there are those for whom time moves slowly; their days are tediously long and they are forever watching the clock and waiting until it is time for bed. Generally, we experience time as moving fast when we are totally absorbed in what we are doing, and slowing up when we are sitting around waiting for something to happen.

Quite apart from our idiosyncratic perceptions of time, there is no doubt that work outside the home has become incredibly stressful with a situation which began with the recession in the 1980s and continues to cause insecurity in the job market. Those who can actually find paid employment are expected to cope with the consequences of cost-cutting and under-staffing. Nowadays, it is not unusual to see job advertisements demanding that applicants 'must be able to work under pressure'. This could be deemed a reasonable request for such people as ambulance drivers or medical staff in the casualty department of a busy hospital. But surely it is an indictment of our times to expect office workers to pump adrenaline as a matter of course.

To help quell stress at work, there is now a huge industry built around 'time management skills'. Workers are sent on courses (sometimes during their lunch break!) to learn how to prioritise and plan their day. True, for many people such courses can make a major improvement to productivity. However, the emphasis on systems misses the point that successful time management is about

motivation not mechanisms. In other words, the motivation to manage your time is more important than the mechanics of time management.

An informal research study headed by psychologist Stephen Williams of Resource Systems (UK) demonstrated this point clearly. Workers were asked to think about the time when they were most effective and achieved a great deal. Consensus of opinion revealed that people were most efficient just before a holiday, when they moved offices or when they changed jobs. 'They haven't changed their systems, suddenly remembered their time management training or picked a day when they have nothing to do', says Williams, 'The difference is one of motivation. They have to clear their desk, tidy up the loose ends and manage their time, so they do it. It's as simple as that.' Indeed, many people surprise themselves by what they can accomplish through the power of motivation. It provides yet another example of the 'mind over matter' phenomenon.

If the concept of time management is new to you (unfortunately, a potentially stress-inducing term!) the following tips will enable you to organise your time more efficiently, both at work and in your personal life. It is taken for granted that you will also be fired with motivation.

Tips for Organising Your Time

✓ Make a 'to do' list, prioritising everything you need to do in terms of urgency and importance. If you have difficulty in prioritising, ask another interested party to help you draw up the list. As well as listing those things you need to do today, you may also find it helpful to include tasks that need to be completed within, say, one week or one month. Also, make a list of long-term projects to be completed within one year. However, do ensure that your goals are realistic and that it is humanly possible to complete the tasks within the allotted time. Otherwise, making 'to do' lists will simply add to any existing feelings of overload

✓ When planning your daily work schedule, attempt to balance routine tasks with more enjoyable jobs, then the sense of achievement will put

▶

you in a positive frame of mind for the rest of the day. However, it is important to stick to one task at a time and finish it.

✓ When dealing with a large project, break it down into smaller jobs and work through each part systematically. However, if it looks as though a deadline has become unrealistic, renegotiate the terms without further delay; for if you leave it until the last minute you may well annoy or inconvenience other people.

✓ You are not indispensible, so stop trying to do everything yourself. Whenever possible, delegate. Ask someone else to do those things which prevent you from concentrating on more important tasks.

✓ Don't say 'yes' to everything. Give yourself time to consider whether you can cope with further demands on your time – and that any new request can be handled with relative ease.

✓ Ensure that you find time each day to be with the people you love. No partnership will flourish without time spent together. If you go out to work, reward yourself for organising your time more efficiently by leaving earlier one night, taking more holiday or not taking work home.

✓ Make a note of social and family occasions, holidays and times when you *must* give priority to family matters – and ensure that you do!

✓ If you spend most of your time in the company of other people, it is essential to capture some time to be alone. This will give you the space to reflect, and to gain perspective on issues both at work and at home. One way to gain this special time is to get up half an hour earlier two or three times a week. This will enable you to make a proper breakfast, take an aromatic bath, listen to music – or maybe to do some yoga stretches and deep breathing exercises. Even though you may feel tired at first, you may also discover that it takes some of the stress out of your life.

THE HARASSED PARENT

If you are a parent looking after children all day, this can be even more taxing than going out to work. The lack of mental stimulus and the absence of social contact may lead to discontentment and depression, which will undoubtedly affect every member of the family. However, it is possible to capture some time to relax (preferably away from the home environment) if you really want to. Although it may mean a juggling act, the reward will be worth far more than the effort expended. As well as enhancing your own mood, the feel-good vibes are bound to positively affect others in your sphere, especially children. As children are so receptive to the changes in mood of their parents, they will respond by becoming more joyful and relaxed themselves.

- Where one partner goes out to work and other stays at home, think of ways in which the employed partner can help with some of the domestic chores and take an active part in child care – perhaps during the weekends.

- Ensure that the partner who is the full-time carer is given some time off now and again to relax and replenish their energies – even if it is simply to lie in a warm bath.

- It can also be helpful to enlist the help of family and friends, perhaps building up a supportive baby sitting network. Sharing the responsibility for minding the children provides you with the opportunity to enjoy an afternoon or evening out with your partner. Or if you are a single parent, it will enable you to visit friends, exercise or do whatever you need to recharge your batteries.

TRANSCENDING MONOTONY

There is also the growing problem of having too, much time available as a result of retirement, unemployment or underemployment. Similarly, tedious employment can create its own form of stress. But whatever the trigger, the lack of mental and physical stimulus – exacerbated perhaps by money worries – can lead to depression and feelings of isolation. If this reflects your own situation, consider the following suggestions.

- If you have an understimulating job but cannot afford to give it up until you find other employment – or if you are generally living in a rut – make every effort to break the daily routine. This may sound obvious, but is easy to overlook when you are feeling despondent. Visit new places as often as possible; follow up sudden notions; take up a new hobby; provide for compensatory physical activity such as walking, cycling, swimming – or even a competitive sport which will give you an adrenalin boost! You may also find it helpful to take the Bach flower remedy Wild Oat (see Chapter 2).

- To ease feelings of loneliness, go to evening classes or join a club or group that centres on your main interests. If you have a fear of meeting people, practise deep relaxation (pages 20–1) or creative imagery (Chapter 6) and/or take the Bach flower remedy Mimulus (see Chapter 2). If you love animals, a cat or dog will ease feelings of loneliness and isolation and will bring joy into your life. Moreover, the act of loving and caring for another living being encourages a more intimate relationship with life itself. However, even though it should go without saying, do ensure that you are able to devote the necessary time and attention to the animal's welfare.

- If you find routine tasks like washing the dishes or doing the housework excruciatingly boring, then transcend the mundane by listening to inspiring music while you work. You may also find it helpful to vaporise energising essential oils such as bergamot, coriander, geranium, grapefruit, lemon, palmarosa, pine, rosemary. (*Instructions for vaporising essential oils are to be found on page 56.*)

- Conversely, you may find it helpful to carry out routine tasks the Buddhist way – through the practice of mindfulness. This means becoming totally immersed in the task, becoming acutely aware of every nuance of movement. By consciously entering into the spirit of work in this way, it becomes an act of meditation. But how can this possibly make light work of a chore? It is impossible to explain it in everyday terms; but through the mysterious workings of paradox, the exercise is incredibly freeing. Try it and see!

● To help alleviate feelings of anxiety, despondency, frustration, boredom, pessimism and apathy – or even to help you find your true vocation in life – the Bach flower remedies can be of enormous benefit (see Chapter 2). Some of the following remedies may be particularly helpful.

─SUGGESTED BACH FLOWER REMEDIES─

Gentian: for those who have a generally pessimistic outlook.

Gorse: for feelings of hopelessness and despair.

Hornbeam: for tiredness and weariness, that 'Monday morning' feeling.

Mimulus: for fear and anxiety.

Larch: for lack of confidence.

Wild Oat: for boredom and frustration, especially in relation to career.

Wild Rose: for apathy.

Willow: for those who constantly dwell on the unfairness of life.

THE SECRET OF HAPPINESS

In the introduction to this book we paid homage to the simple joys of life. Let us return to this theme for a moment. According to Edward Bach, here paraphrased, real happiness is the contentment experienced in small things; doing the things that we really love to do, being with the people that we truly like. There is no strain, no effort, no striving for the unattainable.

One of the most beautiful and healing experiences of all, to my mind, is to watch young children and animals at play. A toddler building sand castles on the seashore, mischievous kittens unravelling balls of wool, puppies playing rough and tumble games, lambs springing on a grassy hillside, dolphins frolicking in the waves – all bring a contented smile to most people's faces.

And finally, I was once asked by a magazine journalist to summarise my formula for a healthy life. My answer? Let go of striving, succeeding, winning and gaining and you will be much healthier and happier. Unfortunately, this view was out of sync with the philosophy of the magazine, and indeed with the mood of the times, and so did not get printed!

Here's wishing you inner peace!

Bibliography

Ackerman, D. *A History of the Senses* (Chapman, 1990)

Bach, Dr E. *Heal Thyself* (C.W. Daniel, 1931)

Blynsky, G. *Mood Control* (Charles Scribner (USA), 1978)

Carr, R. *Yoga For All Ages* (Book Club Associates, 1972)

Christensen, K. *The Green Home* (Piatkus, 1995)

Coghill, R. *Electro-Pollution: How To Protect Yourself Against It* (Thorsons, 1990)

Day, C. *Places of the Soul* (Aquarian, 1990)

Eastcott, M.J. *The Silent Path* (Rider, 1969)

Ferucci, P. *What We May Be* (Aquarian, 1982)

Fincher, S. *Creating Mandalas* (Shambhala, 1991)

Gimble, T. *Form, Sound, Colour and Healing* (C.W. Daniel, 1987)

Goldman, J. *Healing Sounds* (Element Books, 1992)

Graham, H. *A Picture of Health* (Piatkus, 1994)

Hoffmann, D. *The New Holistic Herbal* (Element Books, 1990)

Holford, P. *The Whole Health Manual* (Thorsons, 1981)

Housdon, R. *Retreat* (Thorsons, 1995)

Kenton, L. *The New Joy of Beauty* (Vermillion, 1995)

Kingston, K. *Creating Sacred Space with Feng Shui* (Piatkus, 1996)

Krista, A. *The Book of Stress Survival* (Gaia Books, 1986)

Lake, M. *Scents and Sensuality* (Futura Publications, 1989)

Mabey, R. *Food For Free* (Collins, 1972)

Markham, U. *Women Under Pressure* (Element Books, 1990)

Milner, J.E. *The Tree Book* (Collins and Brown, 1992)

Minter, S. *The Healing Garden* (Headline, 1993)

Nahmad, C. *Earth Magic* (Rider, 1995)

O'Hara, M. *A Song For Ireland* (Michael Joseph, 1982)

Pennick, N. *Earth Harmony* (Century Paperbacks, 1987)

Rimpoche, S. *The Tibetan Book of Living and Dying* (Rider, 1992)

Rosak, T. *The Voice of the Earth* (Touchstone, 1992)

Rosak, T. *Ecopsychology* (Sierra Club Books (USA), 1995)

Schiff, F. *Food For Solitude* (Element Books, 1992)

Seashore, C. *Psychology of Music* (Dover (USA), 1967)

Shealy, C.N. *The Self-Healing Workbook* (Element Books, 1993)

Sheldrake, R. *The Rebirth of Nature* (Rider, 1990)

Spear, W. *Feng Shui Made Easy* (Thorsons, 1995)

Watson, A. and Drury, N. *Healing Music* (Prism Press, 1987)

Webb, M. *The Spring of Joy* (J.M. Dent, 1917)

Weiner, M.A. *Maximum Immunity* (Gateway Books, 1986)

Wildwood, C. *Aromatherapy and Massage* (Element Books, 1991)

Wildwood, C. *Aromatherapy Made Easy* (Thorsons, revised edn 1993)

Wildwood, C. *The Book of Aromatherapy Blends* (Thorsons, 1993)

Wildwood, C. *Flower Remedies* (Element Books, revised edn 1994)

Wildwood, C. *Flower Remedies For Women* (Thorsons, 1994)

Wildwood, C. *The Aromatherapy and Massage Book* (Thorsons, 1994)

Wildwood, C. *Create Your Own Perfumes* (Piatkus, 1994)

Wildwood, C. *The Bloomsbury Encyclopaedia of Aromatherapy* (Bloomsbury, 1996)

Williams, S. *Managing Pressure* (Kogan Page, 1994)

Wills, P. *Colour Therapy* (Element Books, 1993)

Wright, C. *The Wright Diet* (Green Library, distributed by Element Books, 1991)

Suggested Reading

Stress Survival
Chaitow L. *Your Complete Stress-Proofing Programme* (Thorsons, 1993)
Krista, A. *The Book of Stress Survival* (Gaia Books, 1986)

Aromatherapy and Massage
Wildwood, C. *The Aromatherapy and Massage Book* (Thorsons, 1994)
Wildwood C. *The Bloomsbury Encyclopedia of Aromatherapy* (Bloomsbury, 1996)

Creative Blending of Essential Oils
Wildwood, C. *Create Your Own Perfumes* (Piatkus, 1994) (includes advice on blending mood-enhancing room scents).

Bach Flower Remedies
Barnard J. and M. *The Healing Herbs of Edward Bach* (The Flower Remedy Programme, 1988)
Wildwood, C. *Flower Remedies* (Element Books, revised edn 1994)

The Healing Power of Music
Goldman, J. *Healing Sounds* (Element Books, 1992)

Dance Therapy
Natale, F. *Trance Dance* (Element Books, 1996) (comes with a CD of dance music inspired by the native American tradition)

Colour Work
Fincher, S. *Creating Mandalas* (Shambhala, 1991)
Wills, P. *Colour Therapy* (Element Books, 1993)

Creative Imagery
Acheterberg, J. *Imagery in Healing* (New Science Press, 1990)
Ferucci, P. *What We May Be* (Aquarian, 1990)

Herbal Medicine
Hoffmann, D. *The New Holistic Herbal* (Element Books, 1990)

Holistic Healing and Yoga
Chopra, D. *Perfect Health* (Bantam Books, 1990)

Nutrition
Holford, P. *The Whole Health Manual* (Thorsons, 1981)
Wright, C. *The Wright Diet* (Green Library (distributed by Element Books), 1991)

Creating a Healing Environment
Christensen, K. *The Green Home* (Piatkus, 1995)
Kingston, K. *Creating Sacred Space with Feng Shui* (Piatkus, 1996)
Minter, S. *The Healing Garden* (Headline, 1993)

Ecopsychology and Gaian Philosophy

Rosak, T. *The Voice of the Earth*
(Touchstone, 1992)
Sheldrake, R. *The Rebirth of Nature* (Rider,
1990)

Useful Addresses

UK
Essential Oil Suppliers

The Fragrant Earth Co Ltd
PO Box 182
Taunton
Somerset, TA1 1YR
Tel: 01823 335734
Fax: 01823 322566

Phoenix Natural Products Ltd
Southall
Middlesex, UB2 4EZ
Tel: 0181 574 7308

Bach Flower Remedies and Professional Training Courses

The following company produces flower remedies of the highest quality available. They continue to employ the original methods of potentisation as advocated by Dr Edward Bach, using full-strength brandy as a preservative. Please enclose an s.a.e. with all enquiries.

The Flower Remedy Programme
PO Box 65
Hereford
HR2 OUW

Advanced courses in flower therapy:
Clare Harvey
The Shen Tao Foundation
c/o Middle Piccadilly Natural Healing Centre
Holwell
Sherborne
Dorset, DT9 5LW

Aromatherapy and Massage Courses

Hygeia School of Holistic Therapy,
7–9 Springfield Road
Altrincham
Cheshire, WA14 1HE
Tel: 0161 941 5027
Fax: 0161 926 8423

Aromatherapy Organisation

Lists of accredited aromatherapists and professional training courses (please enclose an s.a.e. with all enquiries):

The Secretary
International Federation of Aromatherapists
Stamford House
2–4 Chiswick High Road
London, W4 1TH

Nutritional Therapy

The Institute of Optimum Nutrition
Blades Court
Deodar Road
London, SW15 2NU

Higher Nature Ltd
The Nutritional Centre
Burwash Common
East Sussex, TN21 8ZX

The Eating Disorders Association
Sackville Place
44 Magdalen Street
Norwich
Norfolk, NR3 1JU

Full Spectrum Lighting

If you suffer from seasonal affective disorder (SAD), as discussed in Chapter 3, and would like to obtain full-spectrum lightbulbs or an anti-SAD light-box, contact:

Full Spectrum Lighting Ltd
Unit 1
Riverside Business Centre
Victoria Street
High Wycombe
Bucks, HP11 2LT

Sound Therapy

Information and workshops:

Jill Purce
20 Willow Road
London NW3 1TJ
Tel: 01225 462 450

Music for relaxation:
New World Cassettes
Paradise Farm
Westhall
Halesworth
Suffolk IP19 8BR
Tel: 0198 681682

The Way of Wilderness

If you would like to embark
on a wilderness trip as
described in Chapter 4,
contact the organisation
below – the only such group
in the UK. Alternatively,
contact one of the wilderness
organisations in the USA (see
page 163).

Sahara Walk
The Open Gate
1 Woodman's Cottage
Brockham End
Bath, BA1 4BZ

Counselling and Healing

Lists of accredited
practitioners:

**British Association for
Counselling**
37A Sheep Street
Rugby
Warwickshire, CV21 2BX
Tel: 01788 578328

**National Federation of
Spiritual Healers**
Old Manor Farm Studio
Church Street
Sunbury-on-Thames
Middlesex, TW16 6RG
Tel: 01932 783 164

*Drugs, Alcohol Abuse and
Smoking*

Information and helpline for
families and friends of drug
users – including addiction to
prescribed drugs:

ADFAM National
Chapel House
18 Hatton Place
London, EC1N 8ND
Tel: 0171 405 3923

*Advice and support in
overcoming alcoholism:*

**Alcoholics Anonymous
Helplines** – England 0171 352
3001; Scotland 0141 221 9027;
Wales 01646 69555; Northern
Ireland 01232 681 084

Advice and helpline for
families and friends of
alcoholics (local groups
throughout the UK and
Eire):

Al-Anon
61 Great Dover Street
London, SE1 4YE
Tel: 0171 403 0888

*Advice on giving up
smoking:*

Quit
102 Gloucester Place
London, W1H 3DA
Tel: 0171 487 2858

Bereavement Support

Help and advice plus contact
with other bereaved people:

CRUSE
Cruse House
126 Sheen Road
Richmond
Surrey, TW9 1UR
Tel: 0181 940 4818

Lone Parenthood

Support and advice:

**National Counsel for One
Parent Families**
255 Kentish Town Road
London, NW5 2XL
Tel: 0171 267 1361

USA
Essential Oil Supplies

Essentially Yours
PO Box 81866
Bakersfield
California, 93380
Tel: 805 323 0648

Aroma Vera Inc
PO Box 3609
Culver City
California 90231

Aromatherapy Organisation

Lists of accredited
aromatherapists and training
courses:

**American Society for
Phytotherapy and
Aromatherapy**
PO Box 3679
South Pasadena
California 91031

Flower Remedies and Professional Training Courses

The Flower Essence Society
PO Box 459
Nevada City
California 959
Tel: 916 265 9163 or 800 548

The Way of Wilderness

The following groups have been long established and have made significant, unique connections between wilderness work and ecopsychology:

The School of Lost Borders
Box 55
Big Pine
California 93513

North Star Wilderness
Box 1407
Port Townsend
WA 98368

Breaking Through Adventures
Box 20281
Denver
CO 80220

Earthways
Box 303
Big Sur
California 93920

CANADA
Essential Oil Suppliers

Escents Aromatherapy
1855 Welch Street
North Vancouver
British Columbia V7 1B7
Tel: 604 984 7790

Essentially Yours Canada
960 Parsons Road
Richmond
British Columbia
V7E 1L1
Tel: 604 241 9774

Samarkand Trading Co
(distributors of Fragrant Earth)
1983 West 57th Avenue
Vancouver
British Columbia V6P 1T9
Tel: 800 260 7401/604 267 7433

Aromatherapy Organisations

Institute of Aromatherapy
300A Danforth Avenue
Toronto
Ontario M4K 1N6
Tel: 416 465 3882

Institute of Dynamic Aromatherapy
Jade Shutes
1983 West 57th Avenue
Vancouver
British Columbia V6P 1T9

Herbalists

Thuna Herbals
(qualified herbalists)
298 Danforth Avenue
Toronto
Ontario M4K 1N6
Tel: 416 465 3366

AUSTRALIA
Essential Oil Suppliers

Essential Therapeutics
58 Easey Street
Collingwood
Victoria 3066

In Essence Aromatherapy
3 Abbot Street
Fairfield
Victoria 3078

Aromatherapy Organisations

Lists of accredited aromatherapists and training courses (please enclose an s.a.e. with all enquiries):
International Federation of Aromatherapists
1st Floor
390 Burwood Road
Hawthorn
Victoria 3122

NEW ZEALAND
Essential Oil Suppliers and Accredited Courses

Absolute Essential
PO Box 90539
Auckland Mail Service Centre
93 College Hill
Ponsonby
Auckland
Tel: 09 360 0914

Offers a Diploma in Aromatherapy (accredited by NZQA) as well as several short courses in Auckland, Wellington and Christchurch.

Aromatherapy New Zealand Limited
Clare Anthony Institute of Holistic Aromatherapy
PO Box 47470
34 Kelmarna Avenue
Ponsonby
Auckland
Tel: 09 378 6962

Offers a Diploma in Classical Aromatherapy (accredited by NZQA and the International Federation of Aromatherapists) as well as aromatherapy certificates by distance learning.

Time (Intl) Ltd
(for In Essence essential oils)
PO Box 18–185
Auckland 6
111 Apirana Avenue
Glen Innes
Auckland
Tel: 09 528 5001

Blackmores
(for Culpeper essential oils)
2 Parkhead Place
Albany
Auckland
Tel: 09 415 8585

Index